from

burnt

out

to

fired

up

reigniting your passion for teaching

MORGANE MICHAEL

Solution Tree | Press
a division of
Solution Tree

555 North Morton Street
Bloomington, IN 47404
800.733.6786 (toll free) / 812.336.7700
FAX: 812.336.7790

email: info@SolutionTree.com
SolutionTree.com

Visit **go.SolutionTree.com/teacherefficacy** to download the free reproducibles in this book.

Printed in the United States of America

Library of Congress Control Number: 2021040142

Solution Tree
Jeffrey C. Jones, CEO
Edmund M. Ackerman, President

Solution Tree Press
President and Publisher: Douglas M. Rife
Associate Publisher: Sarah Payne-Mills
Managing Production Editor: Kendra Slayton
Editorial Director: Todd Brakke
Art Director: Rian Anderson
Copy Chief: Jessi Finn
Production Editor: Alissa Voss
Content Development Specialist: Amy Rubenstein
Copy Editor: Kate St. Ives
Proofreader: Elisabeth Abrams
Text and Cover Designer: Kelsey Hergül
Editorial Assistants: Charlotte Jones, Sarah Ludwig, and Elijah Oates

To Makena and Tyson, listen for the whispers in your hearts and trust in your ability to get to where you are destined to be.

Acknowledgments

Many people have contributed to our thinking and rethinking about this work since its conception. We express our gratitude and appreciation to those who have inspired us to give this project a go, encouraged us when we encountered challenges in the process, and reminded us of the value of this book's important message. Thanks to all of you who have served as sounding boards, guinea pigs, and guardrails.

I don't think this book would exist if it were not for the arrival of Makena and Tyson, who catapulted me from my old life to another richer, more three-dimensional version of it. Seeking my place within this new existence, as a teacher and mother, helped me practice the art of *done is better than perfect* and recognize the beauty of true vulnerability. Thank you for the gift. I am grateful for the beauty you both bring into my life through your curiosity, creativity, and pure joyfulness. Makena, your heart is as big as the moon, and your dreams are even bigger! Tyson, your positive light is contagious; keep shining it.

To Geoff, thank you for teaching me so much, for shepherding me into adulthood, and for your partnership as an amazing parent.

To my sister, Kelly, thank you for your fierce courage, encouragement, and shoulder to lean on. You're a gem.

To my C. B. friends, where would I be without the laughs, the memories, the love, and the quotes? No distance will ever truly keep us apart. Jodie, thank you for your unrelenting lifeline consistency on TGIMs ("Thank Goodness It's Monday" weekly 6 a.m. phone calls). Bianca, thank you for your compassionate, listening ear. Megan, thank you for inspiring my sense of authentic creativity through your own example. Deanne, your strength and resilience is admirable and inspiring. Chloe, you're an inspiration in so many ways—you've taught me how to truly show up for others. Ashley, thank you for the laughs and depth.

To the WW Mastermind (Lisa, Linda, Pippa, Kristin), thank you for the deep wisdom, advice, and Zoom conversations that always seemed to replenish my well-being, inspiration, and creativity when I needed it most.

To my ball girls, thank you for the love, advice, care, and memories. Laura, thank you for always being there. Carly, thank you for being a soft landing. Thora, thank you for being real. Kim, I so appreciate your candor and understanding. Jen, thanks for bringing the fun!

To the SJD crew, I am grateful for the open arms and laughter, especially Lauren, Trish, and Sarah.

To Julie, thank you for your unwavering support, for your perspective, and for calling me out with well-timed questions.

To Mom, I am thankful for the way you lit up for me in the early days. I saw my own capabilities through your eyes, and that gave me confidence to dream big, to keep on reaching.

To Kathy, thank you for always having faith and for your listening ear.

To Lynn, thank you for your support and reminding me that it's okay to take the hands off the wheel once in a while.

To all who listen to *KindSight 101* or who hang out on Instagram, Twitter, or Facebook, I see you and I read every single message, text, and email you send. I am grateful for the feedback you've given me, for the positive messages, and for the ability to meet some of you in person. Thank you for believing in the importance of compassion and this journey.

I will forever be grateful to Seth Godin, who gave me a second chance to show up as myself, who is as genuine and kind as he seems, and who has inspired an incredible number of people to reject the "tyranny of 'picked'" so that we can pick ourselves.

Thank you to Elizabeth Gilbert, who kick-started my creative journey through her book, *Big Magic*. That book brought me to life.

To Sarah Jubar, my fabulous editor, for lovingly telling me when my work was terrible and for encouraging me emphatically when it wasn't, in our sidebar conversations. Thank you for being such a delight to work with!

Solution Tree Press would like to thank the following reviewers:

Casey R. Ahner
Director of Instructional Support
Los Lunas Schools
Los Lunas, New Mexico

Allison Cunningham
Instructional Coordinator New
   Teacher Induction Program
Peel District School Board
Mississauga, Ontario

Craig Mah
District Principal of School Services
   and Special Projects
Coquitlam School District
Coquitlam, British Columbia

Jenny McMaster
Special Education Resource Teacher
Sioux Lookout, Ontario

Jamie Nino
Area Administrator
Sanger Unified School District
Sanger, California

Robin Noble
Author and Retired Principal
Santa Fe, New Mexico

Christine Roy
Principal
St. John the Baptist/King Edward
   School
Saint John, New Brunswick

Lynn Thomas
Secondary English Teacher
Grand Erie District School Board
Brantford, Ontario

Visit **go.SolutionTree.com/teacherefficacy** to download the free reproducibles in this book.

Table of Contents

Reproducible pages are in italics.

6 Reignite: Craft Your Own Road Maps to Go From Burnt Out to Fired Up

About the Author

Morgane Michael has been an elementary school educator with the Greater Victoria School District in British Columbia, Canada, since 2008. Michael is a passionate advocate for social-emotional learning, kindness education, and educator well-being, and she leads professional development initiatives aligned with those efforts throughout her province.

Michael pursued her interest in developing positive school culture through kindness and self-compassion practices, by promoting effective social collaboration, by nurturing creativity, and through building self-efficacy that is responsive to students' needs. She established a culture of high expectations by launching her podcast, *KindSight 101*, in 2018. She has interviewed some of the world's biggest names in education on the topics of kindness, well-being, self-compassion, and promoting positive school culture. Michael is also the creator and founder of the Small Act Big Impact 21-Day Kindness Challenge, which seeks to promote and cultivate safe and supportive school culture. She shares insights from her podcast and lesson ideas on her blog, *Small Act Big Impact* (www.smallactbigimpact.com).

Michael received a bachelor's degree in elementary education from the University of Victoria, British Columbia, and is currently completing a master's degree in educational leadership. She lives with her family in Victoria, British Columbia.

To learn more about Morgane Michael's work, visit Morgane's website and blog, *Small Act Big Impact* (www.smallactbigimpact.com), listen to her *KindSight 101* podcast, follow @smallactbigimpact on Instagram, or follow @MorganeMichael on Twitter.

To book Morgane Michael for professional development, contact pd@Solution Tree.com.

Introduction

My heart pounded and my fingertips tingled in anticipation that September morning as I stepped into the musty, ramshackle drama annex for the first time. Somehow, despite its shabby appearance, it was as though my eighth-grade self knew that it would one day become a place of solace and self-expression for me.

Mr. Graham, the school's drama teacher, had a reputation that preceded him. Renowned for being eccentric and, truthfully, a little manic, he became one of the most remarkable teachers I ever had. He spoke in metaphors with a raspy British accent and inhaled Benson and Hedges cigarettes like a chimney just steps from the classroom door. Mr. Graham sported a spectacular assortment of vests and scarves, custom-made, only to be described as a cross between my grandmother's so-bad-they're-good brocade curtains from the seventies and Don Cherry's weekly ensembles on Hockey Night. He was unorthodox and certainly wasn't an administration favorite. No, he was a rule-breaker, and the students adored him for it.

Our jaws dropped the first day in his class when he announced that every single one of us would be learning to juggle. Then, we all just about fell on the floor when he added that we would be expected to memorize Robert Frost's poem, *The Road Not Taken*, and would be performing the juggling and poetry *simultaneously* for our peers. It was audacious to ask a bunch of hormonal preteens to do the one thing they all feared: put themselves on the path of potential public failure in front of their peers. We believed that it was impossible, that we could never do it.

"Of course you can do it," he said, gesturing toward us with nonchalance and a glint in his eye. "You can try. You'll either succeed or fail. And if you fail, fail gloriously!" Then he'd remind us that we could always choose to take the zero (which, surprisingly, nobody ever did). He taught us that it's always better to have tried and failed than not to have tried at all. And do you know what? Somehow, despite our trepidation, most of us succeeded, surprising even ourselves.

Thinking back on it now, the concept of *failing gloriously* is very much in line with Theodore Roosevelt's famous request for people to dare greatly: "It is not the critic who counts. . . . The credit belongs to the man who is actually in the arena, whose face is marred by dust and sweat and blood; who strives valiantly . . . who at the best knows in the end the triumph of high achievement, and who at the worst, if he fails, at least fails while daring greatly" (Thomsen, 2003, p. 11).

My home life as a child was not ideal, and like many children who experience trauma, I would carry the burden of my story with me to school, trying my best to conceal the heartache. Whenever I had dark days, Mr. Graham had a way of making me feel like I belonged, even when I felt like a misfit. On one particularly difficult day in eleventh grade, my shoulders drooped as I made my way toward the drama annex, eyes downcast, flat, and emotionless. Mr. Graham, who happened to be chain-smoking between classes, intercepted me and asked me to wait for him outside. Reopening the door, he extended a hand that held the keys to his vehicle.

"Morgane," he announced with a matter-of-fact tone, "go for a little drive and come on back when you're ready."

Relieved, I remember thinking how kind this gesture had been, knowing that driving off school property was certainly not part of any curriculum, nor would the school have endorsed it. Nevertheless, he had made me feel seen. I was able to escape the confines of school for just long enough to clear my head.

Near graduation, I wrote a few exemplary teachers letters of gratitude and appreciation. Naturally, Mr. Graham was at the top of my list, and although I don't remember the exact wording of my letter, I know I poured my heart out to him.

We stayed in touch after graduation, often going for coffee and catching up. Years later, Mr. Graham called me out of the blue to say, "I'm sick. I've got cancer, and it's terminal." I remember feeling the floor turn to quicksand around me as I processed his words, my mouth dry, a hollowness spreading inside my chest.

It didn't take long before Mr. Graham was too weak to leave his home. One day, he asked me to come over. He didn't have long left. His wife greeted me warmly at the door and guided me down the hallway to the bedroom, where he lay surrounded by pillows. Before stepping into his room, I looked to my right. I stopped in my tracks. There, framed on the wall of the main hallway of his home, was the letter I had written at my graduation.

Small Act, Big Impact

Mr. Graham made a tremendous impact on me, and it was in the moment I spotted my graduation letter hanging on his wall that I learned my words *mattered*. That *I* truly mattered. I realized that I, too, could make a difference. That day, it became my belief that through small, seemingly insignificant acts, I could make a big, positive impact on the people around me. Small act, big impact. After that, I knew I wanted to be a teacher.

Time and time again, I've witnessed the positive impact of daily micro-interactions on the culture of a school. These positive micro-moments enable our *soft skills* (the interpersonal, communication, and self-reflection skills that enable us to be successful in the workplace and in the world) to come to life in an authentic way and they transform the way someone feels at school and about his or her own sense of worthiness as an educator, student, or member of the school community. We've all seen the way a small smile or head nod from a colleague can signal encouragement during a stressful staff-meeting presentation. We've all experienced how clear face-to-face communication can resolve potential misunderstandings and assumptions, leading to more effective and collaborative problem solving. At one point or another, we've all witnessed how flexibility in scheduling and tasks can allow educators to showcase their strengths while enabling them to learn from one another.

By challenging our biases and mobilizing authentic kindness in schools, it is possible to create ideal school cultures of belonging and psychological safety, a weighty goal that I'd say most educators, parents, and students wish to achieve. A strong culture of psychological safety and belonging is built by micro-moments and results in innovative risk taking, sound social-emotional learning practices, and educators and students who not only feel prepared for the uncertain future but who are capable of reaching their fullest potential (Seppälä & Cameron, 2015).

The problem, however, is that these powerful micro-moments are hard to lean into with a whole heart if we, as educators, are feeling stressed out, burnt out, and underappreciated. Demonstrating empathy and compassion, the cornerstone of great teaching and human connection, can feel nearly impossible when we're not first taking the time to extend compassion to ourselves. If educators want to be effective change-makers for our students and within our schools, we first need to take care of ourselves so we can thrive.

Overwhelmed Teachers, This Book Is for You

Have you ever felt disillusioned by the very system you once aspired to become part of? According to the Anxiety and Depression Association of America (ADAA, n.d.b), teachers and students in classrooms across North America are displaying elevated anxiety, depression, and, even worse, suicide rates. In the general population, the ADAA (n.d.a) reports that approximately one in five adults has a mental illness. When it comes to teachers, a 2017 research study from the University of Missouri finds that job-related stress dramatically affects 93 percent of the teaching population, meaning we're a particularly stressed bunch of professionals (Herman, 2018).

Many of you are at a breaking point because of the pressures of state and government testing (especially in the United States). Many of you are feeling *not enough* because of the public call for you to give even more of yourselves than you possibly can. Many of you are experiencing firsthand the daily toxic stress responses due to your own history of trauma. Many of you are feeling the effects of secondary trauma because of the space you hold for your students who have endured heartbreaking stories. Many of you are inadequately compensated and underappreciated for your work in the classroom. Many of you work hard to support students struggling with dysregulation in the classroom, pouring your heart into every lesson and interaction and returning home each day more and more depleted. As educators teaching students within a broken education system, it can feel impossible to meet the many diverse needs of our students and to feel like we're making a positive impact.

If this is how you feel, this book is for you. If you've ever had days where you questioned your efficacy as an educator, this book is for you. If you've experienced some level of trauma in your own life or that of someone close to you, this book is designed to remind you that you are not alone and that you can gain the tools to recharge yourself. If you simply feel overwhelmed and headed toward burnout, this book will inspire you to reignite your passion and purpose.

I want to help you build some positive social-emotional practices around learning self-compassion, creating meaningful connections, and tuning into your sense of purpose. I want to enable you to direct your energies creatively to care for your students and show up for them in a meaningful way without compromising your wellness and sense of wholeheartedness. Together, we will create a plan or road map, designed specifically for you, that can reconnect you to the educator you've always wanted to be.

The truth is, we can't keep burning the candle at both ends and hoping to stay fired up. It takes tremendous resilience and optimism to bounce forward in the face of adversity. This book is full of research-based strategies for educators and administrators to help sustain and replenish their own well-being.

Chapter Overview

The first five chapters of this book focus on the 5 Rs framework, which invites educators to reflect, reframe, refocus, reconnect, and reveal through specific, research-based activities and exercises. The final chapter offers a specific and detailed road map to consolidate and build on your self-growth throughout the book. My 5 Rs framework is inspired by science-backed principles and practices related to personal and professional well-being, connection, and fulfillment and touches on the five core competencies of social-emotional learning established by the Collaborative for Academic, Social, and Emotional Learning (CASEL, 2012): (1) self-awareness, (2) self-management, (3) responsible decision making, (4) social awareness, and (5) relationship skills. Teachers' social and emotional competence (SEC) and well-being play an important role in their ability to contribute to a positive classroom climate (Jennings & Greenburg, 2009). Facilitating a responsive, inspiring, and nurturing school culture requires educators to focus, first and foremost, on their own happiness, creative passions, and sense of well-being.

Reflect

Understanding ourselves and reflecting on our state of mind is an essential component of replenishing ourselves as educators. In a noisy world in which busyness is revered as a status symbol and the number of likes you get on social media masquerades as a measure of your worth, it's increasingly important to pause and evaluate your needs, motivations, and internal narratives in order to take stock of your state of mind.

In chapter 1, you will learn about the positive impact of self-awareness on educator well-being as we explore intentional self-compassion, reflective practices, and gratitude as a means of replenishment. You'll learn the science-backed benefits of taking time to refill your own cup in a go, go, go world and specific ways to do it. Strategies shared in this chapter include writing your self-care bucket list, the happiness jar exercise, a loving-kindness guided reflection, journal prompts, and five specific approaches to mindfulness you can implement anytime you're feeling burnt out as a teacher.

Reframe

Even in some of the most adverse situations, teachers are expected to be flexible, positive, adaptable, competent, and knowledgeable, dedicating themselves to meeting the needs of their students no matter the circumstance. The weightiness of these high expectations, coupled with the personal stressors that arise within our own lives, can take a toll on our well-being. Resilience is an important quality of wholehearted educators, according to resilience researcher and educational consultant Elena Aguilar. Aguilar (2018) asserts that teaching is the kind of work that is inherently stressful and that, in order to not only show up as role models for our students but to also stave off burnout, teachers need to dedicate themselves to forming resilient habits. Within our capacity for self-awareness, we must make room to audit our internal narratives and to reframe them in such a way that we gain the capacity to recover quickly from adversity. Resilience is about reframing our circumstances and making necessary changes so that we can maintain our positivity, efficacy, integrity, and well-being as educators.

In chapter 2, you will learn what research has taught us about the benefits of resiliency and how to adopt a reframe mindset. You'll also examine some of the restrictive personal beliefs that limit you as a teacher. Strategies shared in this chapter include a resiliency journaling exercise, creating positive mantras to reframe your internal self-talk, several exercises on self-regulation to reduce the stressors in your life, and writing a powerful letter to yourself that will serve as a reminder of your strength, potential, and ability to meet adversity with confidence.

Refocus

We all have deep-seated dreams that reside within us, and there comes a time when we must take a good look at our lives to determine what we want our story to be. Goals without the discipline and consistency of daily action often fuel a sense of discontent and a lack of success (Matthews, 2015). Refocusing is your ability to take stock of those dreams and to recalibrate your compass in such a way that you can step into the life you've always hoped to have on a personal, professional, and relational level so you can feel more fulfilled in your role within the classroom. You may not always know where your journey will take you, but you can certainly position yourself in the right direction to reach your potential.

In chapter 3, you will explore what the research says about self-management and responsible decision making and goal setting as well as the internal and external expectations for educators. You'll learn the nine steps of goal setting, highlight five secrets for goal-setting success, and discuss the confidence circles concept (and what it means for educators). Strategies you'll find in this chapter include the painting your future vision-boarding exercise, a goal-setting template, a five-second habit hack that can help you overcome procrastination, and reflection exercises to maximize your productivity and accountability to your goals.

Reconnect

Our interactions with one another, positive or negative, can have a contagious effect on the people who work and learn with us. When we think about being wholehearted in our approach to education, it makes sense to lean into more positive interactions that lead to trust-building, an overall sense of psychological safety, healthy boundary setting, and perspective-taking with colleagues, parents, leaders, and, naturally, our own students.

Humans are neurobiologically designed to connect to one another (Lieberman, 2015). Quite often the very mechanisms that were once designed to protect us—like wanting to fit in or avoid situations that entail risk—no longer serve us. The good news is that, with intention, we can override some of these antiquated systems to become better communicators in this modern time. When we spend most of our lives at school, we should strive to make it a happy place to be, a place where others feel compelled to showcase their true selves and can look to us as positive influencers in their lives.

In chapter 4, you'll explore ways educators can contribute positively to the emotional and social environment in their schools, specifically focusing on developing social awareness and relationship skills. You'll also dig into what the research says about the value of promoting positive morale with colleagues, creating and maintaining authentic connections, and finding belonging and building trust. Strategies shared in this chapter include several simple ways you can build rapport with anyone, an exercise to counteract toxic school-staff culture, three ways to contribute to a culture of trust and belonging in your school, and an exercise on how to give meaningful recognition to those around us while maintaining authenticity.

Reveal

"Oh, I'm not creative." How many times have you heard someone refute their own creativity with a sense of scientific conviction? Maybe you're guilty of doing this, too. Worse, maybe you've disclosed your perceived lack of creativity with your own children or students! Here's the thing—your perceived lack of creativity is total nonsense. Claiming that you're not creative is a mechanism that allows you to hide from the potential of failure.

As Mr. Graham would have said, we need to prepare ourselves to "fail gloriously" on the road to success. We can't protect ourselves from the sting of failure if we want to live big, bold lives. Failure is the key to success (Tough, 2011). For iterative, failure-based learning to work, research indicates that educators and parents need to encourage students to figure out what went wrong and try to improve (Columbia University, 2016). As Xiaodong Lin-Siegler, founding director of the Education for Persistence and Innovation Center (EPIC), states, "Failure needs to give people a chance to regroup and rewind the clock" (Fattal, 2018). Lin-Siegler's primary goal "is to help students realize that failure is a normal part of the process of learning" (Fattal, 2018).

We are all born creative. It is only in adulthood that some of us lose the childlike capacity for divergent (creative) thinking (Massimiliano, 2015). Inviting a sense of play and creativity into our daily practice is an integral method for reconnecting to ourselves and our own well-being as educators (Forgeard, 2015). "Creative activities teach us agency, the ability to change the world, to mold it to our liking, to have a positive effect on our environment," states neuroscientist Daniel Levitin (2014). In other words, creativity allows us to practice the skills we've developed for self-awareness, responsible decision making, self-management, social awareness, and relationship building—the important social-emotional learning domains that enable us to be change-makers, especially in our role as educators.

In chapter 5, you'll explore the concept of *flow*, the research on the value of creativity in schools (specifically for teachers), perfectionism, procrastination, some of the common creativity roadblocks, and the transformative power of sharing our creativity with others. Additionally, this chapter includes a series of specific strategies to foster a creative mindset and to establish strong creative practices, including a curiosity audit to identify your main passions, a fun-filled improvisation game to promote creativity among colleagues, and six personal challenges that encourage creative risk taking.

The Reignite Road Map: From Burnt Out to Fired Up

So many incredible educators, just like you, dedicate themselves to a career in education with the goal of making a positive and lasting impact on the world. It is possible to continue making a difference through your work while maintaining a deep sense of wellness, worthiness, and wholeheartedness. You can be remarkable without burning out!

In chapter 6, you will take all the hard work, exercises, and reflections you've done throughout the book and consolidate them into a personalized, actionable *reignite road map plan* for your future. The reignite road map will follow the framework of the 5 Rs. You will explore each of the 5 Rs through culminating questions, exercises, journal prompts, and reflection opportunities that integrate some of the learning you've already done and take it to the next level for your future. The framework will help you to focus on each of the 5 Rs in a flexible way, either in a linear fashion all at once, bit by bit, or even out of sequence if there is a particular theme that resonates most with you. This is your journey. As you know with your own students, personalizing learning and growth is the most effective way to maximize success. The reignite road map can be accessed, for example, through a monthly book club meeting with your colleagues or collaborative team. Alternatively, you might want to do all five sections in one day, dedicating your-self to professional learning with your colleagues, incorporating discussions and group reflections into the work. You might even want to use the reignite road map as a jump-off for an educational Twitter chat in your district or an online forum. My hope is that you will revisit this plan daily, weekly, monthly, and even yearly so that you can align your actions, your intentions, and your goals to become the educator you've always wanted to be.

Chapter Features

Every chapter will include research on the focus theme and effective strategies related to that topic to ignite your fire. In addition, each chapter will offer teacher, student, and classroom examples in action, to bring the fired-up journey to life.

Throughout this book, I will share personal anecdotes as well as tangible prac-tices from my own life and from educators who have been guests on my podcast, *KindSight 101*, with the goal of helping you to reconnect with yourself, those around you, your purpose, and your creative curiosity. Leadership coach, edu-cator, and speaker Ilene Berns-Zare (2019) said, "Having a purpose—whether large or small, whether we reach the objective or continue to strive for it—informs our existence in important ways that may impact physical and mental health and overall well-being." When we focus on our well-being and purpose through the lens of joy and creativity, we are better able to serve others and ful-fill the greatest expression of who we're meant to be (Alimujiang et al., 2019). Mr. Graham taught me that anyone, regardless of age, has the capacity to make a tremendous impact on others. He has remained in my thoughts as a constant reminder of my potential as an educator and of my desire to make the most of the micro-moments within each day. Now is the time for radical self-care, to take charge, calibrate your compass, and commence the journey to becoming *fired up* so that you can reach your potential as a change-making educator!

REFLECT

How to Tune In and Check Up on Yourself

We do not see things as they are, we see them as we are.

—Anaïs Nin

In order for us to show up to every interaction and micro-moment for our students, colleagues, and stakeholders with a generous, wholehearted spirit, we need to commit ourselves to self-care habits that enable us to give from a place of authentic generosity. Otherwise, we'll burn out.

In this chapter, you will explore what the research says about your need to reflect. You will learn about the adverse effects of teacher burnout, explore how your brain responds to stress, and discover the science behind your needs and emotions. Chapter 1 also includes three essential approaches for developing self-compassion through meaningful reflection exercises. In the second half of this chapter, you'll put theory into practice by discovering several strategies to improve educator mindfulness and self-compassion and reignite your fire for reflecting.

What the Research Says About Reflecting

Questions determine the quality of our lives, the quality of our thinking, and the quality of our teaching. According to Simon Sinek (2014), "When most organizations or people think, act, or communicate, they do so from the outside in, from *what* to *why*. And for good reason—they go from clearest thing to the fuzziest thing. We say *what* we do, we sometimes say *how* we do it, but we rarely say *why* we do *what* we do" (p. 39).

Too often in education, we begin with the *what*. Our curriculum gives us a fairly prescriptive road map in terms of *what* we have to teach. During teacher training, most of us come away with the understanding that to fulfill our mandated obligations to the curriculum, our next goal is to plan our *how. How* do we get to our *what?* The thing is, no matter how good we get at the *what* and the *how*, our true measure of effectiveness and passion as educators lies in our *why* (Mart, 2018). Why do you do what you do every day in the classroom? *Why* did you choose teaching as a profession?

It's likely that you became an educator because of your own positive experiences with a teacher like Mr. Graham or because of negative school-related experiences that inspired you to want to become the teacher you never had. When asked why they became teachers, 85 percent of respondents said it was because they wanted to make a difference in children's lives (Bill and Melinda Gates Foundation, 2014). I'd wager that many others became teachers in order to help children realize their unique potential and become the highest expression of themselves within the context of their unpredictable, exciting future.

Despite the many and varied reasons *why* they enter this profession, countless educators are buckling under the pressures they experience. Although teachers work tirelessly to serve their students, many are not practicing what they preach—and they are burning out. Many teachers are leaving the profession entirely. According to research scientists at the University of Pennsylvania, approximately 46 percent of educators in North America leave the profession within the first five years of their careers, despite having chosen teaching to fulfill altruistic and optimistic goals of making this world a better place (Garcia & Weiss, 2019). These numbers can be much higher in Title I schools (Garcia & Weiss, 2019). Despite the noble cause of making a difference, many educators are leaving the profession in droves, unable to keep pace with the rapidly increasing demands placed on them. Figure 1.1 is a diagnostic checklist you can use to help identify whether you are feeling burnt out or are on your way to being burnt out as a teacher.

The good news is, research indicates that reflection on our current emotional state, followed by adequate self-care practices, can help mitigate the effects of burnout. In their groundbreaking book *Burnout*, Emily Nagoski and Amelia Nagoski (2019) assert that emotional exhaustion, the feeling of fatigue associated

☐ Are you exceptionally tired every morning, even if you've had a good night's sleep?

☐ Does it take you a long time to complete simple tasks?

☐ Are you filled with dread as you look forward to the day ahead or even farther into the weeks, months, and years ahead of you?

☐ Do you feel overworked and overwhelmed at work, or in your personal life?

☐ Are you quick to anger or are you often irritable?

☐ Do you tend to call in sick often or seek ways to get out of going to work?

☐ Do you feel a lack of motivation at work and in your personal life?

☐ Are you having trouble identifying your passion, purpose, and larger life goals?

☐ Are you avoiding things that once brought you joy at work and in your personal life?

☐ Are you overwhelmed by the responsibilities in your life?

Source: Adapted from Maslach & Florian, 1988.

Figure 1.1: "Am I headed for burnout?" checklist.

with continued external and internal stressors, is one of the leading causes of burnout for those within the helping professions, such as teaching. Therefore, in order to combat the effects of burnout, we first need to reflect on our emotional state. Then, we can move through challenging emotions as one would go through a tunnel to get to the light at the end. Nagoski and Nagoski (2019) further argue that emotional exhaustion occurs when individuals linger on an emotion such as resentment, sadness, helplessness, despair, grief, or anger, becoming stuck in that emotion due to circumstance instead of moving through the emotion.

From my experiences, there are two major factors leading to teacher burnout.

1. Failure to adequately practice social-emotional learning (SEL)

2. Primary and secondary stress

In the following sections, you'll learn about the impact of these factors on educators and discover what the research says about how teachers can practice self-care and reflection.

The Paradox of Social-Emotional Learning

Teaching children SEL is my *why* of teaching and is one of the most important things we can do within our classrooms. Through SEL, educators strive to prepare their students to become flexible, manage their complex emotions, set goals, make effective decisions, and nurture positive relationships (CASEL, 2012).

The problem, however, is that many of us, as educators, are not all that good at putting SEL into practice in our own lives. This fact can be detrimental to the effectiveness of our teaching and negatively impact our own wellness. Although mandated SEL programs have been proven to be effective (CASEL, 2012), individual educators ultimately hold the key to preparing students for the future by actively modelling social-emotional soft skills within the classroom walls. Recall that soft skills include the abilities we can successfully develop around critical thinking, problem solving, social interaction, leadership, professionalism, work ethic, and self-awareness. As SEL expert Kimberly Schonert-Reichl (2017) asserts, "Teachers are the engine that drives social and emotional learning (SEL) programs and practices in schools and classrooms, and their own social-emotional competence and well-being strongly influence their students" (p. 137).

Unfortunately, although we work hard to deliver SEL to our students, we often fail to employ those same self-care and social-emotional competencies within our own lives. Stress and poor emotional competence are among the foremost reasons why teachers become dissatisfied with the profession and leave their positions (Darling-Hammond, 2001). In fact, first-year teachers, often underprepared for the realities of the classroom, are not able to recognize mental health issues like anxiety and depression in themselves (Koller & Bertel, 2006).

The High Cost of Stress

Stress is the most cited reason for teachers choosing to leave teaching—in other words, burning out. In a recent survey from the American Federation of Teachers (2017), 61 percent of educators say that their work is always or often stressful, and over 50 percent say that they don't have the same enthusiasm as when they started teaching. Consistent stress can lead to burnout. As workplace stress and burnout expert Christina Maslach explains, burnout is "a psychological syndrome emerging as a prolonged response to chronic interpersonal stressors on the job" and causes exhaustion, cynicism, detachment, ineffectiveness, and lack of motivation" (Maslach & Leiter, 2016, p. 103).

Empathetic Distress

Empathic distress, a term coined by the Buddhist teacher and medical anthropologist Joan Halifax (2018), refers to the self-oriented response to the suffering of others and the desire to withdraw from anything that is causing the distress. Sometimes, empathic distress can contribute to burnout, if a teacher becomes overwhelmed or perceives that he or she is unable to positively affect a student or colleague's difficult situation (Wróbel, 2013). Working with students who are struggling with trauma in their lives when we have limited abilities and structural supports to help them can lead to burnout and empathic distress.

"I felt distress," Rebecca Alber, a Los Angeles-based education professor at UCLA, told me when she remembered feeling overwhelmed in her first few years as an educator when faced with the secondary trauma associated with teaching children with varied and heartbreaking stories. "We can provide . . . a space where [students] feel safe, needed, necessary, wanted, loved, where they can take off their armor. That said, how does that leave us feeling as teachers? Overwhelmed? Hopeless? Anxious? I would go home, and by Sunday, I would feel an anxiousness because I knew I would be checking in on a few students who were in foster care or in a home which was a place where they did not feel loved" (Michael, 2018d).

Self-care and self-compassion practices were the only ways that Alber was able to acknowledge that she was contributing to the best of her ability for these children, but that she had her limitations. She now encourages the teachers in her program, when they experience secondary trauma, to manage some of the stressors through self-compassion, self-care, and clear boundaries. Later in this chapter, we will explore some specific reflective and self-care practices that can contribute to refilling your empty cup.

The compounding effects of stress not only affect an educator's career and ability to make a positive impact but can also have devastating effects on mental wellness. Our presence as emotionally available adults in the lives of our students can be a powerful predictive force contributing to their overall functioning in life, but it's difficult for us to be emotionally available to them if we are experiencing stress ourselves (Miller & McGowan, 2014). Prolonged negative stress can also have adverse effects on our well-being as educators and can even outweigh the known risk of tobacco use, alcohol consumption, and physical inactivity (Cohen, Janicki-Deverts, & Miller, 2007). Stress is consistently associated with poor mental and physical health, including depression and anxiety (Cohen et al., 2007; Slavich, O'Donovan, Epel, & Kemeny, 2010).

As it stands, anxiety, depression, and suicide rates are a concern in North America. According to the National Institute of Mental Health (NIMH, 2021), more than one out of every five people struggle with mental illness. More than three-fifths of Americans self-identify as lonely (Cigna, 2020). Suicide is the second leading cause of death in ten to thirty-four-year-olds in North America (NIMH, 2021). It is time to take educator well-being seriously—our lives literally depend on it.

Our Six Universal Emotional Needs

Most educators are likely familiar with Abraham Maslow's (1943) hierarchy of needs, which asserts that in order to function in society and lead a successful life, five key needs must be met in hierarchical order. Physiological basic needs—such as food, safety, and shelter—need to be met first, followed by our need for belonging and love. Next comes our need for esteem (to be trusted, to be respected, and to have freedom) and self-actualization (to become the truest expression of ourselves).

While I can appreciate the relevance of this framework, first developed in the 1940s, I often felt puzzled by the fact that people can make beautiful, self-expressive creative works of art and still struggle with their most basic needs or their lack of belonging. I'm not the only one who is struck by this. Psychologists Louis Tay and Ed Diener (2011) state that motivation is a pluralistic behavior. A person may be motivated by higher needs despite lower-level basic needs not being met. I couldn't help but wonder, "What *does* motivate our actions?"

According to world-renowned family therapist Cloe Madanes (2016), there are six universal emotional needs that drive our actions and shape our personalities. Human behavior is informed by our inherent need for (1) certainty, (2) uncertainty, (3) significance, (4) belonging, (5) growth, and (6) contribution. People can meet these needs through positive, neutral, or negative means. Often, we are motivated to meet one or two of these needs above all the others. Understanding your own relationship toward these needs and corresponding behaviors can provide some insight into the decisions we make and interactions we have. With self-reflection and clarity comes the possibility of choice. Much of our dysfunctional behavior can be traced back to an inability to meet our emotional needs (Madanes, 2016).

Certainty

It's essential that we feel a sense of security as we take risks and live our lives. When that sense of certainty is threatened, individuals will assert their power and influence on a situation in order to ensure a manufactured sense of predictability.

During the height of the COVID-19 pandemic lockdown, for instance, when it came to online planning throughout the spring of 2020 and our return to in-class learning in the fall of the same year, I felt driven by my need to create certainty in a very uncertain time. Much of my behavior—the list making, the rigid scheduling, the organizing, and my quest for information—was evidence of my attempts to meet the unmet need for certainty.

Uncertainty

Those who seek out uncertainty and variety in their lives are seeking unpredictable outcomes. Often, they are thrill-seekers who are energized by the momentum that comes from having to think and react on their feet. Some of our most memorable experiences can result from those events that fall outside of routine and the norm. When we think of our most unpredictable students, the class clowns and jokesters, often their need for variety outweighs their need to contribute to a calm classroom. Even the most disciplined, routine-oriented teachers, too, seek out variety in their lives. During the summer months, for example, I love to release myself from the rigidity of the school routine for at least a few days and spend unstructured time at the beach playing with my children or travel to new destinations without a clear itinerary in mind. Variety adds a sense of excitement and welcome unpredictability to life.

Significance

Those who seek out significance have a need to feel unique and important. They want to matter, to be seen, and to feel like the work they do matters. Often, recognition can be enough for them to meet the need for significance. Teachers often spend many of their extracurricular hours marking, coaching, preparing, and collaborating to provide powerful learning opportunities for their students. While most don't tend to do these things for acclamation, it sure feels good to feel recognized for the efforts we put forth.

Belonging

Often our need to belong and connect with others can result in rewarding relationships and interactions (Eisenberger & Cole, 2012). Current research supports that we are neurobiologically wired for connection and belonging. Humans are driven to seek social acceptance through fitting in, and our brain's reward circuitry reinforces this by releasing the happiness hormone, dopamine, when we do. Brené Brown explains in her book *Braving the Wilderness* (2017),

> "True belonging is the spiritual practice of believing in and belonging to yourself so deeply that you can share your most authentic self with the world and find sacredness in both being a part of something and standing alone in the wilderness. True belonging doesn't require you to change who you are; it requires you to be who you are." (p. 40)

When it comes to teachers, belonging can feel like having a colleague to vent or laugh with, someone who really *gets* your perspective. It can look like walking into a new school and being welcomed by new colleagues and administrators. You can feel a sense of true belonging when you know that the personal gifts and talents you contribute to your school community are appreciated and valued by those within it. Feeling a sense of true belonging also allows us to make our voices heard during stressful staff meetings, aligning ourselves more with an inner sense of integrity than the worry of not fitting in.

Growth

Humans are motivated by a need to grow, to achieve progress in our own lives (Fink, 2013). Many teachers, for example, are driven by a need to keep learning, creating, and working hard to gain mastery over our curriculum and find new, innovative ways of connecting with our students. Sometimes, however, the downside to taking on ambitious performance goals can be that we sacrifice our much-needed rest and healthy habits (Moeller, Theiler, & Wu, 2011).

Contribution

Most educators enter the profession out of a desire to make a positive impact on the world around them. Although generosity is arguably one of the most important soft skills associated with communication, collaboration, and workplace success (Grant, 2013), it can be easy to forget about giving ourselves the gift of self-compassion.

Tuning into our needs is one part of the self-reflection puzzle. To know ourselves, we need to reflect on the complex emotions we feel, especially when we feel like we are close to burning out. We need to create space for reflection within our downtime as educators—even if it's only for a few minutes a day—in order to know ourselves and live our lives with intention.

The Need for Space to Reflect on Our Emotions

Cultivating space to reflect is not always an easy thing to do, but it is essential to carve out a small amount of time to allow for introspection and self-reflection, especially as a generous educator who dedicates so much of your time to others. As we've learned, educators and those within the helping professions (nurses, doctors, medical professionals, and educational assistants, among others) often experience emotional fatigue caused by balancing the extreme stressors within their professional and personal lives (Nagoski & Nagoski, 2019). Reflecting on our emotions allows us to identify them, which, in turn, provides us the opportunity to consciously move all the way through the emotions, instead of staying stuck within them (Nagoski & Nagoski, 2019). Living with a sense of emotional *stuckness* can lead to burnout; therefore, emotional reflection and self-awareness enable us to mitigate the potential of burnout before it has a chance to affect us deeply. Some simple ways to create small moments for reflection in your day include the following.

- Take a short walk.

- Wake up five minutes earlier than usual.

- Head to bed a few minutes earlier than usual.

- Take an extra moment to reflect during your morning shower.

- Set your alarm for a three-minute reflection at lunchtime.

An important part of tuning in and reflecting comes down to being able to identify, name, and observe some of the complex emotions we experience without self-judgement. Our feelings provide us with important information. If we don't intentionally drown out the figurative noise in our lives and *get quiet*, it's difficult to get to the root of what our feelings are trying to tell us about ourselves and our internal state. Some of our emotions are easier to recognize and accept than others, but all humans experience some version of each universal emotion on the spectrum. Universal emotions can include the following.

- Happiness

- Joy

- Sadness
- Grief
- Anger
- Disappointment
- Fear
- Excitement
- Guilt
- Shame
- Gratitude

Our emotions can be very complex. Joy, for example, can be one of the most positive emotions, but it can be difficult to embrace (Brackett, 2019). How common is it to be experiencing joy because you've just landed that new teaching contract, earned that specialty certificate, finished another year of teaching, or had a really positive interaction with your principal or a challenging parent? Does that nagging little voice creep in to remind you to guard against the bad experiences that may follow your current state of joy?

Sadness and grief can deepen our understanding of and compassion for others and enrich our own lives, but as with joy, these are not emotions humans tend to lean into willingly. Being left out socially, feeling sadness, and experiencing grief in fact cause us the same level of distress and discomfort as physical pain (Kross, Berman, Mischel, Smith, & Wager 2011).

In Western culture, we tend not to speak about sadness and grief because they are socially taboo (Kuehn, 2013). In a 2008 interview with journalist Barbara Platek, psychotherapist and author Miriam Greenspan asserts that there is an alchemy that occurs when we are grieving, in which we surrender to the experience of being split right open and eventually get to a place where we recreate who we are within the experience of that grief (Platek, 2008). She states, "Grief is a teacher. It tells us that we are not alone; that we are interconnected; that what connects us also breaks our hearts—which is as it should be" (Platek, 2008). Although it feels impossibly painful to allow sadness and grief to pass through us, allowing the waves of grief to ebb and flow as they are meant to is the best thing for our recovery from a difficult event.

Fear is also a complicated emotion. Evolutionarily, fear signaled to us to stay safe and mobilized our limbic system to release adrenaline that would enable us to fight, flee, or freeze (Brackett, 2019). If we didn't have the capacity for fear, we would forgo establishing classroom safety rules and routines, we wouldn't bother bringing first aid kits on our field trips, we wouldn't censor ourselves with parents and superiors, and we wouldn't worry about playground supervision for our students—but fear doesn't always serve us well these days. Often, fear is maladaptive because it prevents us from doing the very things we need to do to be successful in the modern world, like speaking in front of crowds, standing out from others, and taking creative risks at work (Rosen & Donley, 2006). Our bodies physiologically process fear and excitement in exactly the same way. A helpful way to reframe our fearful anxiety can be to think of it as excitement (Gross, 2015).

Anger, too, can be a difficult emotion. I recently spoke with a teacher friend and mother of three who asserted, "I wasn't really an angry person, *per se*, until I had my own children. Something about the pitch of their voices when we're in our morning rush routine really triggers me to flip my lid." She told me, "I often wind up yelling at my kids on our morning commute or during the bedtime routines, and it honestly makes me feel awful. I have a low threshold of tolerance sometimes, especially when I'm stressed." Often, anger stems from a belief that we are being treated unfairly or that we've experienced injustice (Brackett, 2019). For many parents and teachers, the burden of our everyday responsibilities can feel overwhelming and unfair, triggering an anger response. This feeling of constant anger can be a sign that we're heading toward burnout.

Guilt and shame are complex emotions with surprisingly opposite outcomes depending on how we contextualize a situation. Imagine you're working on a professional development seminar for your school with a coworker. You've both worked really hard to prepare a presentation. One of your responsibilities was to prepare the PowerPoint for the presentation. You forget to save the file onto your computer and, as a result, your coworker is not only disappointed but also upset at you because without the slideshow your presentation will fall flat, reflecting badly on both of you and making you seem unprepared.

According to researcher Brené Brown (2010), there are two ways you might respond to this conundrum that reflect whether you have a shame-based mindset or a guilt-based mindset. If you feel shame, your immediate thought pattern is that you're a *bad* person. You might say to yourself, "I'm the worst co-planner ever. I am such a loser for forgetting that PowerPoint." Shame is the belief that "I *am* bad." Shame is a focus on self and can leave you feeling like there is something inherently wrong with you that prevents you from accessing belonging (Brown, 2010). Our self-talk really matters and often frames the way we move through our relationships. Shame is highly correlated with aggression, addiction, depression, suicide, bullying, and eating disorders.

If, however, your reaction is "I *did* something bad," you're feeling guilty. Guilt is a focus on behavior instead of one's inherent character and traits. It is the ability to separate who we are from our actions without degrading our worth (Weingarden, Renshaw, Wilhelm, Tangney, & DiMauro, 2016). If your self-talk sounds like, "Oh boy, I can't believe I did that. That was a terrible thing to do. I made such a poor choice to not back up my work!" you're experiencing guilt. You're able to identify the common element of humanity embedded within your experience and mistake. Guilt is inversely correlated to these same outcomes (Brown, 2010). It's much better for our mental health to focus on behavior, even when we're speaking in jest about ourselves.

Reflecting on your emotions enables you to take stock of your current internal state, which helps you determine what you need and where to go next on your wellness journey. The reality is that it is impossible to feel happy all the time. Emotions can be messy and difficult to understand, but one of the most important aspects of knowing yourself is getting familiar with all your emotions, whether you like them or not. As Daniel Siegel (2014) said, when it comes to the challenging emotions, you have to "name them to tame them."

Reflect on Your Feelings

Take some time to name your feelings every day, even multiple times per day. You can set your alarm three times a day to develop a thoughtful reflective practice. If it feels foreign to checkin so frequently, ask yourself the following three questions and write your responses in a journal.

1. What emotions am I feeling right how?

2. Where do I feel it in my body?

3. What do I need right now?

The Three Secrets to Self-Compassion

Leaning into your role as a wholehearted educator decreases the damaging effects of burnout. Doing so starts with your ability to be self-reflective and accepting of your emotions—good, bad, and human. Reflection and self-awareness integrate a self-compassion practice within your ability to name the emotions you feel.

According to leading self-compassion educator and researcher Kristin Neff (2021), self-compassion means that "you realize that suffering, failure, and imperfection is part of the shared human experience." Self-compassion has three main components. First, self-compassion begins with a strong mindfulness awareness to identify and take note of your own internal state, especially in suffering and stress. Second, self-compassion enables you to be nonjudgemental and show unconditional kindness to yourself. Third, self-compassion practice enables you to identify with your common humanity when you are in the hardest moments in your life, instead of turning inward and isolating yourself from humanity.

The Scientific Benefits of Self-Compassion

There are several physiological and psychological benefits to self-compassion, including the following (Neff, 2011).

- Overall well-being
- Reduced anxiety, depression, and stress
- Increased happiness, curiosity, optimism, creativity, and positivity
- Better physical health
- Lower cellular response to stress
- Reduced cortisol (stress) levels
- Healthier heart rate
- Improved interpersonal and work-related relationship interactions
- Reduced fear of failure
- Increased motivation
- Feeling less overwhelmed in stressful situations
- Resiliency

Developing Mindful Awareness

When we practice mindful awareness, we observe our mental state without judgement, without over-personalizing the beliefs and feelings we experience. Practicing mindfulness is one of the best ways to tune into and learn about our motivations, thoughts, beliefs, personal narratives, and desires (Cardaciotto, Herbert, Forman,

Moitra, & Farrow, 2008). A seemingly simple but challenging concept, it can be helpful to think of it as a practice, not a destination.

Showing Kindness to Self

To show compassion for others, we must have the capacity to treat ourselves with compassion first (Neff, 2011). When you mess up or are struggling, do you tend to treat yourself in the same way you would a friend or a child in your classroom?

If we can show ourselves tenderness and understanding in moments of suffering, in times of perceived failure, or when we believe that we are not enough, we can become more resilient to life's upsets instead of being mired by our own negative self-talk (Neff, 2011). Truly inhabiting an abundant mindset, in which we are able to overcome the challenges life presents us, starts with a capacity to be tender with ourselves, not to be our own worst critics.

Identifying With Our Common Humanity

Kristin Neff (2021), author and cofounder of the nonprofit Center for Mindful Self-Compassion, asserts, "Self-compassion recognizes suffering is part of the shared human experience. The pain I feel in difficult times is the same pain that you feel in difficult times. The triggers are different, the circumstances are different, the degree of pain is different, but the basic experience is the same." The feeling of being alone within our pain amplifies our pain.

Often, when we are struggling, we might engage in comparative suffering, which is the act of comparing our own suffering to that of others and evaluating the suffering according to arbitrary measures (Neff, 2011). For example, at the beginning of the year, it can be common practice to compare your class configuration with that of a colleague's and note the number of students you have compared to theirs. Many of us begin the year feeling underprepared, which we make worse by visiting social media—it's easy to get caught in the negative cycle of comparing our efforts to another teacher's heavily curated highlight reel. During report card time, too, it's easy to compare our lack of productivity with that of our colleagues, each person jockeying to win the title of "top procrastinator." Complaining doesn't change reality—as good as it feels in the moment, it's counterproductive. It's okay to acknowledge our hardships, but we don't want to circle the proverbial drain too long. When it comes to the tough stuff, we have two choices in life: (1) change what we can by taking action, or (2) learn to accept the things we can't change. We can gain perspective about our own situations by reminding ourselves that there are likely others in a similar circumstance, tapping into a common sense of humanity. Additionally, complaining to our spouses about our lack of work-life balance compared to theirs rarely results in an empathic and productive response. We should not measure and compare suffering. Doing so only serves to disconnect us further from others. Recognizing the universal nature of suffering allows us to tap into our common humanity, to acknowledge our need for healing connection.

When you want to connect yourself to a deeper connection to humanity, ask yourself the following:

- Is it possible that my struggle could be similar to someone else's? How so?

- How might this moment of struggle help me gain a greater sense of empathy or perspective, or learn a valuable lesson that I might apply at a later time with others?

- How can I accept the challenges I am experiencing right now as an example that life is meant to be imperfect and a little messy sometimes?

- How might I lean on others to help me through my challenge right now, in such a way that I feel more connected to my community, family, social network, and friends?

Instead of isolating ourselves because we believe that there is something fundamentally flawed about us, it can be helpful to lean into our common humanity and accept our imperfections.

The Power of Gratitude

Gratitude is one of our most potent and powerful emotions. Studies have shown that when we practice gratitude consistently, we experience physical benefits, such as a stronger immune system and lowered symptoms of stress (Sansone & Sansone, 2010); psychological benefits, such as more joyful, positive emotions and an overall sense of happiness (Gan, 2020); and social benefits, including more compassionate behaviors, more helpful reframing of negative situations, and fewer feelings of loneliness (Lambert, Clark, Durtschi, Fincham, & Graham, 2010). When we give pause, notice the good things, and appreciate the things that we generally take for granted—like water, food, shelter, family, friendships, and our daily comforts—we are reminded that life can be good.

According to Robert Emmons, Jeffrey Froh, and Rachel Rose (2019), leading researchers on gratitude, there are two main components that comprise a sense of gratitude. The first component includes the acknowledgment of goodness. We can see that there are things for which to be thankful despite or within the presence of hardship. Despite the utter exhaustion at the end of a busy week as an elementary school educator, I often feel lucky to be in the presence of children who have a unique perspective on learning about the world. The second part of gratitude is identifying the root, or source, of the good. I am reminded of the almost magical nature of learning something for the first time because I get to witness that magic every day in my classroom, and it positively impacts my own perception of my experiences in the classroom. Being able to affirm the source of good reconnects us to our common humanity in a deep and meaningful way.

Establishing a gratitude practice is one of the most beneficial acts we can take to be happy in life (Cherkowski & Walker, 2013). Like self-compassion, gratitude has been proven through countless research studies to have an overall physiological benefit to those who practice regularly by increasing our overall sense of happiness, life satisfaction, and appreciation for our current circumstances (Ackerman, 2021). For educators, cultivating a sense of gratitude is particularly beneficial because it helps us to remain optimistic and positive with our students despite any challenges we might be facing in the classroom or outside of it (Howells, 2014). Not only does a positive mindset enable us to feel happier on a personal level, the trickle-down effect is a benefit to our students as well (Howells, 2014). Unfortunately, there is currently a gratitude gap. It turns out that, on average, only 52 percent of women and 44 percent of men regularly practice gratitude (Barsade & Gibson, 2007).

Strategies to Ignite Your Reflecting Fire

This section of the chapter includes several mindful awareness strategies, a collection of exercises to practice showing kindness to yourself, and three journal prompts that will help you tap into your common humanity.

Mindful Awareness Strategies

Mindful awareness enables you to reflect in a nonjudgemental way on your surroundings, emotions, and circumstances. A more detached perspective enables you to respond to life in a more thoughtful, emotionally regulated, and deliberate manner.

This section contains the following mindful awareness strategies.

- 5, 4, 3, 2, 1 grounding technique
- Three good things exercise
- Reflective counting strategy
- Explore the environment exercise
- Guided gratitude practice

5, 4, 3, 2, 1 Grounding Technique

This grounding technique utilizes the five senses to tap into the present. Whenever you feel stressed or overwhelmed, this strategy will prove helpful—and no one need even know you're doing it (Najavits, 2002). Start the six-step process by taking a deep breath in through your nose and out through your mouth. Repeat three to five times until you feel some calmness and centeredness in your body.

1. **Look:** Look around for five things that you can see and name them.

2. **Feel:** Check in with your body and think of four things that you can feel.

3. **Listen:** Take a few seconds and allow yourself to listen for and identify three sounds.

4. **Smell:** Find two distinct smells that root you into the present. If it's hard to do, move around, or try and remember and name your two favorite smells.

5. **Taste:** Say one thing you can taste. It may be the toothpaste from brushing your teeth, or a mint from after lunch. If you can't taste anything, then say your favorite thing to taste.

6. **Breathe:** Take another deep breath or two to end this practice.

Three Good Things Exercise

Martin Seligman (2011), one of the original thought leaders on positive psychology, shared this meaningful gratitude and mindfulness strategy. There are multiple benefits of this four-step strategy: you engage in self-reflection, you train your brain to search for the good in every day, and you raise your overall happiness and well-being, according to neuroscience (Caputo, 2015). And you can't argue with science!

1. Every evening, before settling into bed, take about five minutes to reflect on your day.

2. Recall three good things that happened in your day.

3. In a journal or even your phone, record the three good things that happened.

4. Repeat the process every night.

Every day, you'll become more aware of the positive experiences you have because you'll feel accountable to yourself every night.

Reflective Counting Strategy

While stress can make it challenging to give your best effort in the classroom and manage your personal life, research has found that breathing exercises can help you regain a sense of calm within the chaos (Seppälä, Bradley, & Goldstein, 2020). When you're stressed, angry, or anxious, the *thinking* part of your brain—the prefrontal cortex—has difficulty responding in socially appropriate ways, making rational decisions, and regulating the expression of your emotions. Thoughtful, slow breathing can initiate a calming effect on your body, slowing your heart rate and stimulating your parasympathetic nervous system (returning you to a more restful, logical state). You can do the following seven-step exercise in just a few minutes, and it will help you hone a mindful awareness through breathing.

1. Start by sitting comfortably, eyes open or closed.

2. Take note of your surroundings, becoming aware of your breathing.

3. Ask yourself, "Where do I feel the rising and falling?"

4. Without changing the tempo of your breathing, notice the shallowness or depth of your inhale and exhale.

5. When you feel ready, start counting each inhale up to a count of ten.

6. Then, start back at zero and count to ten again as you exhale.

7. Repeat this cycle seven to ten times, until you feel a sense of peace within your mind and body.

It's easy for your mind to become distracted by thoughts, so restart the count once you reach ten to keep your mind from drifting.

Explore the Environment Exercise

Developing mindfulness habits can be as easy as immersing yourself in nature. Simply *being* in the great outdoors boasts some significant benefits, including reduced cortisol (a stress hormone) in our bloodstream, increased happiness (Capaldi, Dopko, & Zelenski, 2014), better heart health, improved emotional self-regulation, less conflict and aggression, and a deeper sense of gratitude (Bratman, Daily, Levy, & Gross, 2015). So, give yourself a mindfulness break, head outside, and give this easy seven-step exercise a try.

1. Venture to your favorite place somewhere out in nature.

2. Take a big breath in through your nose and out through your mouth until you feel a sense of centering in your body.

3. Look around yourself and reflect on the vastness of nature around you, in an almost childlike way, for a minute or two.

4. Ask yourself: "What inspires a sense of awe within me right in this moment?" "What is surprising to me right now?" "What gives me joy when I look around me?"

5. Keep breathing. Pay attention to your breath for a few cycles and notice if your breath is shallow or deep, fast or slow.

6. Focus on a small area of your surroundings and ask yourself the same questions but limit your noticing to a small area perhaps the size of your hand on the ground, on a tree, or within a patch of pebbles at the beach. Ask: "What inspires a sense of awe within me right in this moment?" "What is surprising to me right now?" "What gives me joy when I look around me?"

7. Keep breathing. Take note of your breathing again. The feeling of insignificance when we remember that we are just one of nature's creations is awe-inducing and strangely comforting and reminds us not to take ourselves too seriously.

As an educator, you have the capacity to see the world through the eyes of children, just by experiencing nature with them. It's good for them, but it's also good for you.

Guided Gratitude Practice

This thirteen-step guided gratitude practice takes about three minutes and fills you with a sense of gratitude and mindful awareness. It's a great way to start your day, especially if you are dealing with a particularly stressful situation (Robbins, n.d.).

1. Begin by sitting down, legs crossed, eyes closed. Inhale deeply through your nostrils for a count of four and then exhale forcefully through your mouth for another count of four.

2. Begin by thinking of a problem that has been nagging you in your teaching or personal life that on a scale of zero (stress-free) to ten (most stress possible) causes you stress at about a level seven or above.

3. As you think of this stress, place your hands on your heart. Breathe deeply into your hands.

4. As you're breathing, think about the gift of your heart. Feel the strength of your heart.

5. Ask yourself: "What fills you with pride that your heart has helped you to do, to feel, to enjoy?"

6. As you continue to breathe, feeling the beat of your heart, remind yourself: You were loved enough to be given the gift of life. As your heart beats, notice the beauty of your life, recognizing the gift you have within you.

7. Think now of a moment for which you can feel deep gratitude. Remember the moment as though you were there: Feel what you would have felt. Hear what you would have heard. Breathe like you would have if you were there. See what you would have seen in that moment. Soak up the moment of gratitude.

8. Think of another moment of gratitude. It could be a small moment or a simple thing. It could be the way the air feels on your skin. Breathe it. Feel it. Imagine that you were transported to that moment.

9. Now, think of a third moment for which to be grateful. Step into it. Feel it. See it. Hear it. Be there.

10. Now, think back to that challenging situation or conflict that causes you stress. Continue breathing and feeling the deep sense of gratitude.

11. Ask yourself: "What do I know for sure?" "What do I need right now?" "What is my next best step?"

12. Trust that you intuitively know how to proceed. Trust it. Feel it.

13. When you're ready, open your eyes with a renewed sense of peace.

Self-Compassion Strategies

The following is a collection of actionable, easy-to-incorporate ways to practice self-compassion. This section presents the following self-compassion strategies.

- Self-care action list

- Happiness jar exercise

- Loving-kindness guided reflection

- The healing power of soothing self-touch exercise

Self-Care Action List

As an educator, it can be easy to feel overwhelmed by all the things you need to do for others—lighting up for your students as they walk in the door; planning, prepping, and writing report cards; attending countless faculty meetings; engaging in meaningful professional development; keeping up on assessments; connecting with colleagues; coaching; running lunchtime clubs; spending your own money on classroom supplies; making dinner; and driving your own children to soccer practice, among others. This three-step exercise is an invitation to intentionally dedicate some time to self-care practices.

1. Reflect on some of the things you like to do that make you feel replenished or more aligned with where you want to go, or that enable you to gain the much-needed self-reflection time you need to recharge. Begin with a journal and a pen. It might be helpful to think of different categories: individual reflection, connection with others, health and fitness, creative pursuits, and goal-oriented self-care. Write everything down that comes to mind. You might find that some tasks are organizational in nature but that they ultimately allow you to get closer to a goal (for example, organizing your garage, make-up drawer, or medicine cabinet). It may seem like work, but ultimately, organizing your home space can lead to daily happiness (Rubin, 2019).

2. When you're feeling low, go through your list and select tasks that seem achievable and meaningful for you, considering your current circumstances.

3. Reflect on your mood after you've done one of the activities you selected. You can even journal about it. You may have favorites that stand out for you and become part of your daily feel-good routine.

When you are starting to feel a little burnt out, as indicated by the checklist in figure 1.1 (page 13), all you'll have to do is ask yourself, "What do I need right now?" and select something to do from your self-care action list. See figure 1.2 for an example self-care action list.

Move my body: Boot camp, runs, exercise videos, walks

Make something: Writing, painting, drawing, planning a new unit, arranging furniture

Listening and learning: Podcasts, audiobooks, music

Nature time: Beach time, skiing in the wintertime, walking in the forest.

Friend time: Visits with friends, dinner out, paddle boarding at the lake

Quality family time: Camping, movie night, playing at the park

Novelty: Signing up for a new class, traveling somewhere, learning a new skill

Personal care: Getting hair done, getting nails done, having a massage

Reflecting: Journaling, recording a host-on-mic interview, having a deep conversation

---

Figure 1.2: Example self-care action list.

Happiness Jar Exercise

Often, what you need most to counteract the negative thoughts inside your head is a positive reminder of your successes and wins. The five-step happiness jar exercise serves as a personal reminder of the gifts you bring to the world, something you can draw upon when you're feeling low, stressed, or overwhelmed.

1. Make a list of your strengths. Here are some prompts if you're having a tough time coming up with some.

    a. What are some kind things people say about me?

    b. What have I done lately to positively impact someone in a small or big way?

    c. How does my voice matter? How do my actions matter?

    d. What are some of the common ways that people compliment me?

    e. What makes me proud of myself?

2. Have a dedicated place to keep a record of these strengths and accomplishments. This could be a real glass jar, a notebook, or even the Notes section on your phone. What's important is having a dedicated space to keep your thoughts.

3. When you're feeling depleted, take a look at your happiness jar and reflect on your awesomeness.

4. Every time you celebrate an accomplishment, celebrate a big milestone, or receive a compliment, make sure to add it to your happiness jar.

5. Every year—perhaps on New Year's Eve, at the end of the school year, or at the beginning of a school year—pull out your jar and think about all the positive ways you have been impactful this year.

Loving-Kindness Guided Reflection

Sometimes, when you're feeling burnt out or stressed, you just need a moment of focused optimism and structured positive self-regard. The practice of loving-kindness meditation, popularized by leaders in meditation practices, such as John Kabat-Zinn (2018) and Sharon Salzberg (2014), have been effective as a means of rewriting the inner monologue into a more positive, compassionate one.

It is an essential act of love to learn how to be alone with yourself (Kabat-Zinn, 2018). Reciting mantras can initially seem a little uncomfortable and even a bit robotic if you're not accustomed to doing them, but there is something subconscious that happens when you speak positively about yourself over and over and over again that reprograms some of the underlying critical beliefs you have about yourself (Salzberg, 2014). So, when you make mistakes or experience failure, you can sit with the dark feelings of sadness, grief, and anger, while at the same time operating from a deeper understanding that you are worthy of love and belonging despite the mistakes you make. Try the following ten-step exercise.

1. Start by sitting or lying with your eyes open.

2. Take a deep breath in through your nose and out through your mouth. Repeat several times until you feel settled and a sense of calm wash over you.

3. Close your eyes if you feel comfortable doing so.

4. Take note of the way your body connects with the floor below you or the sensation of the chair beneath you supporting your body.

5. Start by sending loving-kindness to yourself. Here are some phrases you can use. (Feel free to change the wording of the phrases to something that resonates with you.)

    a. "May I live with comfort, happiness, and good health." (Repeat three times)

    b. "May I be happy, may I be healthy, may I be free from all pain." (Repeat three times)

6. Now, mentally send your loving-kindness to someone you love or someone who has been kind to you. Keep this person at the forefront of your mind as you recite the following phrases.

    a. "May you live with comfort, happiness, and good health." (Repeat three times)

    b. "May you be happy, may you be healthy, may you be free from all pain." (Repeat three times)

7. Then, mentally send love to a neutral person, keeping the person in your mind as you recite the phrases again.

8. Next, mentally send loving-kindness to someone who challenges you, reciting the phrases while keeping the person in the forefront of your mind. This does not mean you condone past wrongdoings against you or other parties. Rather, it is about being compassionate in your regard for all living things, including those who have done harm. This one can be tricky, but it is a practice.

9. Finally, extend your love to all living things.

10. Open your eyes when you feel ready and reflect on how you feel. Ask yourself, "How do I feel right now?"

The Healing Power of Soothing Self-Touch Exercise

Soothing and supportive self-touch is one of the ways you can calm your nervous system and help support your well-being, especially when you are feeling sad, angry, or overwhelmed by a multitude of emotions (Weze, Leathard, Grange, Tiplady, & Stevens, 2007). The following three steps may guide you through soothing and supportive self-touch.

1. Practice holding your hand over your heart, cupping your hands around your face, or even wrapping your arms tightly around your body.

2. Give yourself a little squeeze.

3. Take a few expansive breaths.

This simple practice can be enough to soothe your stressed nervous system and bring your *thinking* brain (the prefrontal cortex) back online.

Journal Prompts to Help You Tap Into Your Common Humanity

The following are three journal prompts for tuning into your common humanity, especially when you're feeling alone or overwhelmed. Mindfulness awareness is an important first step in becoming self-compassionate. You can be preemptive about developing your mindfulness practice. In your journal, take a moment to reflect on the questions contained in the following three steps.

1. Acknowledge your stress by asking the following questions.

    a. "What is causing me stress, pain, or suffering right now?"

    b. "What is causing me discomfort right now?"

    c. "How is that stress affecting my body? How is that stress affecting my thoughts?"

    d. "What do I wish could be different?"

2. Remind yourself that you are not alone.

    a. Ask, "What are some ways that others might be struggling like me right now?"

    b. Ask, "Who are some of the people who might be experiencing suffering like mine?"

    c. Finish the prompt by saying, "I am not alone in this struggle because . . ."

3. Use a tender tone with yourself. Take a moment to imagine yourself in the third person. Imagine that you were giving yourself advice and encouragement.

    a. What would you say to yourself?

    b. What type of language and tone would you use to convey comfort, safety, and tender encouragement?

    c. What advice would you give yourself, from this third-person perspective?

    d. What would you say to encourage yourself?

    e. What tender wish do you have for yourself?

Conclusion

Cumulative stress can result in burnout, which can leave educators feeling ineffective, purposeless, and even cynical about their personal and work lives. Burnout is detrimental to ourselves and to those around us. As we've explored throughout this chapter, people are social creatures, wired to learn from one another and connect deeply through shared experience. Stress responses and maladaptive self-preservation strategies can interfere with our ability to connect with one another in meaningful ways, nurture healthy learning communities, and live out our lives in intentional, wholehearted ways.

It is essential, therefore, that we learn to reflect on our emotional needs as well as notice and name our emotions so that we can develop the self-awareness to be thoughtful and responsive within our roles as educators. The key to being successful, happy, and fulfilled teachers and human beings begins with our ability to reflect on our current circumstances and to practice self-compassion by developing mindful awareness, showing kindness to ourselves, and tapping into our common humanity, especially when we are struggling. Knowing and accepting ourselves creates the necessary foundation for positively reframing our circumstances in preparation for moving forward.

REFRAME

How to Be Resilient in the Face of Adversity

Between stimulus and response there is a space. In that space is our power to choose our response. In our response lies our growth and freedom.

—Unknown

We've all felt it: the desire to be perfect. However, perfectionist tendencies often do more to hurt than help us. As Brené Brown (2010) has said, "Perfectionism is the belief that if we live perfect, look perfect, and act perfect, we can minimize or avoid the pain of blame, judgement, and shame. It's a shield . . . it's the thing that's really preventing us from taking flight" (p. 56). Perfectionism makes it hard for us to respond in healthy ways, to express ourselves authentically, to cultivate healthy relationships, and to demonstrate self-compassion—all important factors that contribute to well-being (Vandraiss, 2017). The paradox of perfectionism is that it fundamentally separates us from others. Striving for perfection draws us away from authentic belonging, the ability to be who we are without apology, and that human element that makes us relatable to others.

Under the weight of high expectations, challenging classroom situations, and personal stressors, many educators develop maladaptive coping mechanisms such as fight, flight, and freeze (Skinner & Beers, 2016). To be self-aware and live wholehearted lives, we have to unlearn some of the unfortunate lessons we've learned through struggle (MentalHelp, n.d.). We must find new ways to reframe our stories and more helpful coping mechanisms to serve us through difficult times. Doing so is the key to resiliency (Aguilar, 2018).

In this chapter, you will learn about the research related to reframing and resiliency. You will explore how to counteract the restricting beliefs that can hold you back from feeling like the best version of yourself. This chapter includes several exercises that will encourage resiliency, improve your internal self-talk, reduce the stressors in your life, and reframe your mindset.

What the Research Says About Reframing

As many educators experience firsthand, burnout can prevent us from being able to step into the ideal version of our life story. The juggle of everyday life can feel too overwhelming and even shameful to address and change. We can become exhausted and tightly wound as we try to keep it all together. The myth of inadequacy can cause us to push beyond our own limits, often to the detriment of our families, passions, and self-care (Maslach & Leiter, 2016). Conversely, living a life unfulfilled can also sink us deeper into the symptoms of burnout, despair, and lack of motivation, a repetitive feedback loop that can be challenging to circumvent (Brooks, 2013). Burnout begets burnout.

Although so much of what happens to us is beyond our control, we have the capacity to craft our own narratives to live the lives we truly envision for ourselves. We can reflect and become intentional about the lives we wish to lead, but we must begin by exploring our internal monologue and our own level of resilience.

What Is Resilience?

Resilience is the ability to overcome challenging times. In their book, *Option B*, Adam Grant and Sheryl Sandberg (2017) describe resilience as the rapidity with which one recovers from adversity. According to the research of leading psychologist Susan Kobasa, resilience is characterized by people who see adversity as a challenge, who commit to dedicating themselves to their lives, and who acknowledge the limits of their control and take action upon those things within their control (EssayHub, n.d.). The three elements that help with resilience are as follows (Kobasa, 1979).

1. **Challenge:** Resilient individuals see challenges as a *challenge*, not as an insurmountable event. They see a challenge as an opportunity for positive change.

2. **Commitment:** Resilient individuals commit to a personal sense of purpose that permeates all facets of their lives.

3. **Personal Control:** Resilient individuals put their efforts where they can feel empowered and in control. They don't waste time perseverating on circumstances that are out of their control.

In other words, resilient educators see difficult times as moments and opportunities for growth and learning. They commit themselves to make the best of their lives, in all facets of their lives. Additionally, resilient people understand that things may happen to us that are far beyond our control; therefore, it is essential to put our efforts into tasks and experiences that empower us to feel like our best selves, instead of resigning ourselves to feeling helpless, powerless, and ineffective.

The Kindness Ninja

Allie Apels (@joysofkinder), an Alberta-based kindergarten teacher and the founder of the international Kindness Ninjas SEL movement, was faced with one of the most challenging groups of students she had ever taught in her fourteen years as an educator. Many of the students in her class had experienced unimaginable trauma, required exhaustive interventions, and needed safety plans just to attend school (Michael, 2019g). Regardless of her usual optimistic outlook, Allie felt discouraged and worried about the trajectory of the school year.

Allie, her teaching partner, and the classroom educational assistants tried all the mainstream SEL programs and interventions known to them. Despite their experience, this team was unable to affect the challenging behaviors exhibited by so many of their students. The classroom environment did not feel safe, and it was time for a radical solution.

Allie and her team vowed not to give up. They knew that this challenge presented an opportunity for professional growth and learning. Allie brainstormed with her team and finally came up with a brilliant way to encourage the development of a kind and supportive classroom. They introduced a kindness ambassador: the Kindness Ninja. Every day leading up to Christmas break that year, their class would be greeted by the Kindness Ninja, who would leave the students notes and various random acts of kindness missions to complete (which she, herself, would create before class).

Allie explained that the experience was completely transformative for both the adults and students in the classroom that year. The edginess and

continued →

magic of the little ninja fighting for good resonated with the students. The students moved throughout the school and community, fulfilling purposeful kindness challenges and making a positive mark on those around them. They went to neighboring classrooms, their city's senior center, the hospital, the local town hall, and animal shelters, spreading kindness. The students began to see themselves from a new, more positive perspective. Allie and her team committed themselves to the belief that the students' behavior and the classroom environment would improve with time, consistency, and opportunities to practice kindness.

Negative, unsafe behaviors decreased, and the cohesion of the classroom increased. By January, the students insisted that their kindness work continue. Throughout the rest of their time together, the class pulled together as a team, and that year became one of Allie's most memorable and favorite years as a teacher. The experience reinforced her belief that despite difficult circumstances, it is always possible to feel empowered through our actions.

Developing resilience in the face of adversity is like the process of alloying metals (Encyclopedia Britannica, n.d.). *Alloying* is a specific process through which two or more metals are exposed to extreme heat and melted together in a precise combination to form a new, often stronger version of the metal. In this analogy, our challenges represent one metal, and our overall lived experience represents the other metal. Fusing the two experiences together allows us to develop perspective. Adversity allows us to forge ourselves like metals into more dynamic, stronger, more beautiful versions of who we are meant to be and enables us to create foundations for others and build a new future for ourselves.

The Three Essential Keys to Resilience

So, what is the difference between resilient people and those who get bogged down by their challenges? Martin Seligman (2011), founder of positive psychology, states that there are three mindsets that predict resilience and the ability to bounce forward when it comes to adversity or a difficult set of circumstances.

1. **Personalization ("It's all my fault"):** People who encounter difficult times may tell themselves that they are to blame for the hardships they endure. Instead, resilient individuals tend to recognize that challenges are part of life and not their fault. When we blame ourselves for the

adversity in our lives, we personalize the struggle, making it hard to separate ourselves from the shame we feel about the struggle itself. Do you often find that you blame yourself for the hard knocks you experience in life?

2. **Permanence ("I will always feel this way"):** Permanence is the belief that things will stay static and will never change, and that, somehow, you will always feel the way that you do in this moment. When it comes to challenging moments, permanence can take the form of despair. Despair is the belief that things will always be as bad as they are now (Bell, 2020). When we are struggling, it can feel impossible to believe that the struggle will ever end. When you believe that your circumstances can change, you develop a more resilient mindset. *Hope* is the belief that there will be a better tomorrow. Where you are right now in your life does not have to be where you remain. Tell yourself, "This is temporary. This will not last forever. I can get through this tough period."

3. **Pervasiveness ("Bad things always happen to me"):** Pervasiveness within the context of adversity is the belief that "bad luck always happens to me." It is the deeply held belief that bad luck will permeate every corner of your life and that you are predestined to be a victim to it. To be resilient, we need to find the sliver of what's good in our lives and cling to that with intention. What's good in your life right now?

Educator Resilience

When it comes to addressing the pervasiveness of teacher stress and retention, resilience is important (Harmsen, Helms-Lorenz, Maulana, & van Veen, 2018; Kelchtermans, 2017). Educator resilience depends on a few key factors, including gratification on the job, dedication to the role, effectiveness, ability to stay engaged and motivated, overall healthy mindset, and optimism (Mansfield & Beltman, 2019). Additionally, teachers can develop many of these indicators of resilience during their preservice training (Gibbs & Miller, 2013). Therefore, it is important for postsecondary institutions to provide explicit resilience training and extensive social supports during teacher education programs (Mansfield, Beltman, Weatherby-Fell, & Broadley, 2016). (BRiTE, which is available at www.brite.edu .au, is an example of an online resilience-building tool that offers resilience training.) Researchers find that preservice teachers with strong social support networks, positive connections with colleagues, and good relationships with their students demonstrate a higher degree of resilience, job satisfaction, commitment, efficacy, sense of optimism, and overall motivation (Mansfield & Beltman, 2019). As they moved into their independent, professional roles as classroom teachers, mentorship (pairing between new teachers and experienced teachers) also had a positive impact on educator resilience (Day & Gu, 2014).

Finally, the long-term resilience of educators depends largely on their own social-emotional competence *and* the culture and climate of the school in which they work (Mansfield & Beltman, 2019). This means, in part, it depends on strong postsecondary instruction, social networks, and mentorship at the preservice level. As educators move into their role as professional classroom teachers, self-efficacy, social-emotional competence, and school culture contribute to their resilience, which means teachers need to make time to develop these behaviors that support resiliency through ongoing professional work.

Recalibrating After a Crash

It was November 2010, and Janelle Morrison, a teacher turned ultra-marathoner and pro-athlete, was driving down the highway on her way from Kelowna to Calgary for a Spin-a-Thon fundraiser. As she drove, an oncoming van plowed head-on into her vehicle and hurled it (with her inside) thirty feet down an embankment. Janelle lay unconscious for three and a half hours as paramedics worked to extract her from the wreckage. She was airlifted to the ICU, where she was placed into a medically induced coma for ten days.

When she awoke from her coma, she learned that surgeons had performed miracles on her body. She recounted, "I had a shattered tibia and ankle, a broken pelvis and femur, and a fractured vertebrae. My stomach had moved into my chest and moved my heart over, and I had a ruptured diaphragm, punctured lung, a broken arm, and a concussion. I was a mess. I was really broken" (Michael, 2019h).

Some moments can dramatically shift the trajectory of the lives we imagine for ourselves, and we need more than gratitude to pull us through into a place of growth. Racing and teaching had been a lifeline for Janelle. Now, she was just lucky to be alive. She told me, "The surgeon said, you're not going to race again, Janelle, and you'd be lucky if you walk again."

In that moment, Janelle knew it was time to make a big, bold decision about what to do next. She could allow someone else's mindset to limit the hopes she had for her own life, or she could choose an alternative path. "I remember having a full belief and awareness that I would race again, and if there was anything I could do, if there was anything I could say about my future, I was going to do so!" Janelle remembers. She spent the next two years in physical recovery, re-creating a relationship with her body and learning to trust it again through countless hours of exercise and rehabilitation.

Two years later, not only was Janelle walking, but she had also earned third place in her division in an Ironman competition. Although the accomplishment of racing again meant a lot, she learned that self-compassion and self-nourishment were so important to her overall well-being as an individual. "I wasn't feeling fulfilled by the comeback," she said. So, Janelle turned inward and asked, "What do I need right now?" She learned to get quiet through yoga, honoring her need for reflection and self-nourishment. Her resilience is reflected by Seligman's *3 Ps* framework: she knew the crash wasn't a *personal* failure, she believed the effects were not *permanent*, and she knew in her heart that bad luck would not be *pervasive* throughout her life.

Janelle now has a newfound sense of self-compassion and a rejuvenated appreciation for life and shares her wisdom with others as a yoga teacher and personal life coach. Sometimes, to push forward, you need to slow down.

Restrictive Self-Perceptions and Beliefs

The way we perceive our reality is framed by our point of view, which has been cultivated over time through our experiences and our beliefs about ourselves and the world. It is estimated that we process between 50,000 and 65,000 thoughts per day (University of the Sunshine Coast, n.d.), many of which are subconscious. As James Allen (1951), author of *As a Man Thinketh*, writes, "Your beliefs influence your actions." If our beliefs about ourselves are positive, it's more likely that our actions will tend to align with these positive beliefs and, therefore, manifest more positive outcomes (Sisgold, 2013). If, however, our self-perception is negative, our actions (or inaction) may result in less desirable outcomes. Table 2.1 (page 44) provides specific examples of positive and negative beliefs.

TABLE 2.1: EXAMPLES OF SELF-LIMITING BELIEFS VERSUS BELIEFS OF SELF-EFFICACY FOR EDUCATORS

Self-Limiting Beliefs (Negative)	Self-Efficacy Beliefs (Positive)
I always have to be strong in front of my students. They are counting on me, and I can't let them down.	I can show up to every situation in my classroom with integrity and honesty.
I can't ask my colleagues for help. That's a sign of weakness.	It is courageous to ask for support from my fellow teachers and administrators and those who care about me.
I can't make time for myself; I have a lot of planning to do. My students are more important than I am.	My self-care is important. I need to take care of myself to be my best self for my students.
My efforts are never good enough. My classroom isn't as creative as my neighbor's.	I am doing the best I can for my students. That is enough for me.
As a teacher, I am not [creative, firm, fun, connected, fit, knowledgeable] enough.	I am proud of my efforts to be the best that I can be in the classroom.
In order to be loveable, I need to [be more fun, be more social, achieve more, work longer hours, be funnier, be more serious].	I am worthy of love and belonging, just as I am.

For example, imagine that you hope to one day teach grade 3, but you've always been a middle school teacher, so you do not have the experience to teach at this level. A grade 3 job comes up at your district. If you have positive beliefs about your ability to fulfill the role (that despite lack of experience, your passion and dedication would make you an ideal candidate for the job), you might be more likely to apply and possibly get the job. If you have a negative belief system founded on your supposed inability to pull off teaching grade 3, you probably wouldn't apply (and, subsequently, you'd have a 0 percent chance of actually getting the job).

Your mindset and belief system can have a significant impact on the outlook you adopt in life and on the opportunities that arise as a result.

Shame Shields

Our limiting beliefs often stem from maladaptive survival mechanisms (Wadsworth, 2015). Evolutionarily, when we humans find ourselves figuratively alone, the reward circuitry in our brain screams at us to smarten up and find our way back to the tribe—to fit in at all costs (Shamay-Tsoory, Saporta, Marton-Alper, & Gvirts, 2019). This connection-seeking mechanism was very useful to us in the caveman days, because being an outcast meant we were no longer protected from environmental dangers by the group—and the chances of dying were pretty high. The feeling of aloneness is often associated with shame or with the feeling of being unworthy of love and belonging (Brown, 2013). We are programmed for survival, and shame puts our connection to others in danger, which is a threat to our very survival (Suttie, 2016). So, many of us spend most of our lives trying to reduce any possibility of finding ourselves alone and exposed (Shen, 2018). Often, our desire to avoid shame at all costs can result in some maladaptive practices that cause us more harm than good.

Dr. Linda Hartling (Hartling & Luchetta, 1999), author and Human Dignity and Humiliation Studies Director at the World Dignity University initiative and Dignity Press, explains that when we face feelings of shame, we often use three main maladaptive coping mechanisms to protect ourselves from the pain of our experience: (1) moving away, (2) moving toward, or (3) moving against. We might move away from the pain by silencing ourselves, living in secrecy, and ultimately avoiding connection (flight). For example, picture Natalie, a shy child who hides behind her hair and drawstring hoodies whenever she is challenged in mathematics. We might tend to move toward it (freeze) through pleasing, appeasing, and perfecting. For example, think of Jordan, a boy who always wants to do the right thing and frequently asks for reassurance that his answers are correct. We might tend to move against it, hurting people before they hurt us, lashing out in anger, or blaming others (fight). For example, imagine Braxton, a child who consistently responds to conflict situations by blaming others. Fighting back may be the easiest way he has learned to cope with conflict and stress. As these children grow to become adults, it's hard for them to change their habitual responses when triggered or stressed (Shonkoff & Garner, 2012).

Our patterned maladaptive emotional responses to stress can feel like a comfortable default setting, comparable to that cozy old sweatshirt you live in on the weekends. Studies reliably find a strong link between shame and the experience of post-traumatic stress disorder (PTSD) following a traumatic event. If our stress response is triggered on a recurring basis as children, our flight, freeze, and fight reactions can become habitual responses to any sort of stress in adulthood (Shonkoff & Garner, 2012). In fact, some trauma survivors have difficulty regulating emotions such as anger, anxiety, sadness, and shame—and this is more pronounced when the trauma occurred at a young age (Dvir, Ford, Hill, & Frazier, 2014).

It can be easy to subconsciously overgeneralize an extreme reaction as a one-size-fits-all approach when faced with stressful situations. In other words, we learn to avoid processing the pain of shame and corresponding sense of unworthiness by galvanizing ourselves against it in a way that corresponds to our flight, freeze, and fight responses. For example, conflict can be tough to navigate for many of us. Assessment and reporting have the potential to cause conflict with students and parents, especially if a student is not meeting curricular expectations. When you know that your assessment will be met with aggression (such as an angry parent email or a student angrily confronting you in class), it might feel easier to avoid the conflict by elevating the mark. Unfortunately, this approach is one way of fleeing from the stress of potential conflict. Instead of being honest, ethical, and transparent, we've avoided the conflict altogether, exemplifying a flight response. In the context of trauma, PTSD is not considered a mental illness but rather a psychological injury (Carrington, 2020). What's significant and hopeful about understanding PTSD as an injury and not an illness is that even if we suffer the effects of PTSD as a result of lived trauma, we have the capacity through hard work and rehabilitation to overcome the negative effects of our trauma. We do not have to be shackled to and limited by our traumatic experiences forever. It is possible to become resilient after trauma, and much of our ability to bounce forward comes from the narratives we create as we process painful experiences.

Although these protective mechanisms shield us from pain at the outset, they stop serving us in the long term (Wadsworth, 2015). It can be hard to take off the comfy sweatshirt (namely, our patterns of maladaptive emotional responses). This maladaptive emotional shield can prevent us from showing up as our full selves, resulting in a counterfeit representative of who we are.

Toxic Positivity

Striving to develop a positive outlook and belief system should not eclipse or cause us to deny our inherent human emotions like grief, sadness, anger, shame, and disappointment. These emotions serve an important purpose in our self-expression as human beings, indicating when it is time to step back, observe ourselves with some authentic curiosity, and choose how we wish to proceed (Rodriguez, 2013).

The insistence that people should *always* aim to "see the bright side" of their struggle is called *toxic positivity*. Toxic positivity refers to a mindset that seeks out only positive thoughts and rejects the existence of negative emotions and experiences. "Toxic positivity can be described as insincere positivity that leads to harm, needless suffering, or misunderstanding," says psychiatrist Gayani DeSilva (Gillespie, 2020). Not only is it annoying to be faced with toxic positivity when you are truly going through a challenging time, but the effects of toxic positivity and the corresponding concealment of emotions have been proven to have a negative impact on overall mental well-being (Gross & Levenson, 1997).

Educators can experience toxic positivity within their peer-to-peer relationships. For example, imagine it's your end-of-week physical education class and you are refereeing a spirited game of basketball. Suddenly, a scuffle breaks out between two players on the same team. You quickly rush to break it up. Suddenly, you feel the blow of a closed fist on your cheek and realize that one of the students has just accidentally punched you in the face. As you recount the situation to a colleague through tears after school, your colleague responds by saying, "At least your nose didn't start bleeding—that would have been worse!" Minimizing difficult situations is toxic and decreases a person's sense of feeling heard and understood.

Toxic positivity can show up in our teacher-administrator interactions, leaving us feeling disillusioned and frustrated. Imagine it's the beginning of the year and you have a busy classroom, but you've managed the behavioral challenges well so far. The teacher next door also teaches the same grade as you but has been less successful with classroom management. Two new students at your grade level arrive at the school flagged by outside agencies as students with significant needs. Your administrator decides you should be the one to take on the two new students because of your experience, skills, and current success. You object, but your objection is met with "*You* can do hard things. I know *you* can do this! Thanks so much for helping me out with this one." In this circumstance, it would be easy to feel as though you were being punished for your previous successes and even taken for granted. Validation and equity go a long way to feeling valued!

Sometimes teachers can demonstrate toxic positivity with their students even when they're trying to be encouraging. Take, for instance, a teacher attempting to cajole a consistently struggling student by saying, "Look, all you have to do is just keep focusing. You'll get this eventually. Just keep trying your best!" Though it's a nice thought, it's likely that the student's inability to succeed at the task has less to do with his or her focus and more to do with brain-based learning and processing difficulties that are out of his or her control. An entirely different approach is probably needed, not simply a renewed injection of willpower and focus. There are times when encouragement does more to harm than help the student's self-efficacy.

Suppressing emotions through toxic positivity can be more damaging than simply allowing ourselves to work through uncomfortable emotions as they arise.

Five Markers of Toxic Positivity (Quintero, n.d.)

1. Concealing your honest emotions or denying others the right to express theirs.

    Example: Imagine that your friend and colleague was hired for a district position that you wanted, but you don't allow yourself the opportunity to feel privately disappointed that you weren't picked for the position.

2. Trying to move on before you're ready, or expecting someone else to.

    Example: A colleague apologizes for a rude comment he made to you during a class placement meeting and expects you to move on quickly after the apology. You're still feeling hurt, but you try to ignore it and move on.

3. Minimizing someone's lived experience or your own. When responding to someone's bad-news story, starting with "At least . . ."

    Example: Imagine you've had to make a call to Child Protective Services because of a tough disclosure a child has made in your class. After doing so, you're feeling saddened by the situation. Your administrator tries to make you feel better by saying, "At least you only had to make one of those calls this year, right?!"

4. Giving someone advice instead of validating her feelings. Brushing your own feelings aside and moving immediately to pragmatism.

    Example: You're venting to your spouse about a misunderstanding you've had with a student's parent, which has left you feeling like you've got loose ends to tie up. It's the weekend, so resolution is out of reach until Monday. Your spouse responds by telling you what you should have done differently in the first place and how you should approach the problem on Monday.

5. Making others feel badly about the feelings they have. Feeling ashamed of your own feelings.

    Example: Imagine you've had a hard day with your class and you're feeling overwhelmed. You share your feelings of overwhelm with a colleague, who responds by telling you that you really need to be less negative and simply "choose joy."

The reality is that it is impossible to feel happy all the time. The peaks and valleys offer a variation in our emotional landscape, a universal richness in our experience that ultimately leads us to a capacity for empathy and deeper wisdom (Rodriguez, 2013).

Growth Mindset and Reframe Mindset

Being able to respond to the stimulus around us in a thoughtful and deliberate way that aligns with our values and internal wisdom comes from the understanding that we have the capacity to *adapt* to our environment and that we can *choose* to interact in an intentional way. We have the power to take what we experience and reframe our experience in such a way that it truly serves us, instead of allowing our default responses to take over. We can adopt a *reframe mindset*—the ability to respond in a mindful way to our circumstances.

The reframe mindset concept is inspired by the concept of *growth mindset*, coined by Carol Dweck (2006). Growth mindset is the belief that most of our basic abilities can be developed through dedication and hard work. Dweck identifies two mentalities: *fixed* and *growth* mindsets that human beings adopt at an early age and that are ultimately responsible for much of our successes, failures, and happiness.

When it comes to resilience and growth mindset theory, it is possible to dismiss some of the systemic processes and institutionalized mechanisms that function to prevent certain individuals (those from a certain race, social hierarchy, or sexual identity, as well as those with specific individual circuitry and brain chemistry) from overcoming adversity. As Stefanie Faye Frank, a neuroscience researcher and clinician, asserts in her interview on *KindSight 101*, "Growth mindset is not always readily accessible to everyone" (Michael, 2018e). Certain things can hold us back from developing a growth mindset. Frank claims this concept is overgeneralized and has morphed into a buzzword within the field of education, which results in people taking it to the extreme (Michael, 2018e). She calls this *hyper belief*, top-down extremism, whereby we believe so wholeheartedly in the idea of mind over matter, the notion that we can change the architecture of our brain just by willing it so, that we dismiss the reality that environment has a tremendous formative impact on brain development.

The problem with top-down extremism, as Frank states in our 2018 podcast interview, is that "it is a dangerous path because it can create a sense of apathy in society" (Michael, 2018e). Moreover, in a learning culture where we often urge our students to embrace their failures and love their mistakes, growth mindset has the potential to take the onus away from the teacher and the need for his or her approaches to be adapted for each individual student within the class. In other words, it can create the conditions through which people feel as though they don't need to address poverty, racism, trauma, and other barriers to success in people's lives. For educators, this set of beliefs can be particularly problematic within communities that are faced with extreme adversity from poverty, racism, and identity-related inequities. When we begin to believe that people who are living in extreme poverty just have to believe in themselves, it creates a judgement of their inability to overcome adversity and minimizes their legitimate struggles within the political and social circumstances within which they exist.

As educators, we must be aware that some individuals are born into situations that put them at a disadvantage, which makes it exponentially harder for them to simply overcome through sheer will. We need to acknowledge that our environment legitimately impacts our ability to bounce forward with ease and rapidity.

When it comes to resilience, a reframe mindset is an effective outlook to adopt because it acknowledges the fact that we can learn to become resilient and that we can apply new ways to respond to the difficult challenges in our lives, as opposed to defaulting to fixed, reflexive behavioral patterns. Resilience is grounded in the knowledge that living involves mistakes, pitfalls, and missteps (Moser, Schroder, Heeter, Moran, & Lee, 2011). Life can feel uncomfortable, just like learning. A reframe mindset is hopeful and rooted in the belief that we can bounce forward if we have the right tools and outlook, no matter the obstacles that arise in our lives.

When we encounter difficulties, we are offered not only the opportunity to return and bounce back to where we were, but the possibility to *bounce forward* with more perspective, strength, and wisdom than we had before the challenges (Tedeschi & Calhoun, 1996). The concept of *bouncing forward*, also called post-traumatic growth, is a concept that researchers in the field of positive psychology find exemplifies true resilience (Discovery Health Channel and American Psychological Association, 2020). Bouncing back suggests returning or springing back to your state of being before adversity, while bouncing forward represents the transformative effect of adversity on your psyche, outlook, and belief systems.

As we bounce forward and develop the ability to respond to our circumstances in a mindful way, we are prepared to adopt a reframe mindset.

How to Adopt a Reframe Mindset

As educators, we experience challenges such as the devastating effects of burnout, the loss of a loved one, a difficult coworker or unfortunate administrative dynamics, a shattering diagnosis, divorce, or any number of other trials that can push us to the brink of sanity. During these times of struggle, it's helpful to have an approach that can help us through the hard times. While reframing doesn't change the situation, choosing how we perceive the struggle can empower us to bounce forward (University of the Sunshine Coast, n.d.). How we respond to the hardships we encounter is what determines our character (Duan & Guo, 2015). Character itself is built within the micro-moments of survival and recalibration. Reframing our situations begins with seeking the opportunities within each challenge, leaning into our positive beliefs and vision for ourselves, and propelling ourselves forward (Duan & Guo, 2015).

Seek the Opportunity Within the Challenge

Within every hardship is the opportunity for growth, self-learning, and transformation. Much of our resilience comes from our perception about our hardship (Konnikova, 2016). The more you can lean into the positive aspects of the challenging experience, the less pain you'll feel long term (Fredrickson, Tugade, Waugh, & Larkin, 2003). Is this easy to say? Sure. You can't just wish your pain away. It's important to allow yourself to process the feelings of disappointment within your life; nevertheless, in order to move forward, crafting a powerful narrative that attributes growth and learning within the struggle is essential for your well-being (Fredrickson et al., 2003).

For instance, suppose you are a kindergarten teacher in an inner-city school. A child in your class, who has experienced extreme trauma, becomes so frequently dysregulated that she is a daily flight risk (such that she often runs from the classroom and school grounds), consistently lashes out violently at her peers, and regularly rips the classroom apart (tears the books from shelves, topples chairs, and throws classroom books). Part of your role as a classroom teacher is to stay calm, request help from your school team, co-regulate with the child, help create a safe space for the other children who have witnessed her outbursts, and model understanding forgiveness toward the child. Naturally, this requires immense emotional resilience, a skill that will ultimately serve you in the long term, equipping you to face any myriad of challenging classroom experiences. One way to frame the challenge positively is to think, "I am building the important skill set necessary for facing any classroom situation. I am helping this child by being a soft landing for her. I am helping the other children to learn that adults can keep them safe." Although it's hard to practice this way of thinking, finding an empowered sense of meaning within the challenge is truly the key to your emotional freedom. What story are you telling yourself about the hardship? What are the opportunities within the challenge?

Lean Into Positive Beliefs About Yourself

Part of recalibrating yourself after a challenge comes from you own self-awareness. Think back to some of the mindful awareness strategies in chapter 1 (page 26) to help you set the tone as you reflect on the questions, What are my strengths? What do I believe about my current experience? What do I need most right now?

Imagine you're a middle school teacher who is expecting your first child. The first six months of the pregnancy journey have been less than ideal; you've been sick every single day, the odor sensitivity has become extreme, and your emotions have been unpredictable. On this particular day, swimming through the clouds of pungent cologne spray and body odor in the halls has brought you to a breaking point. In between classes, you find yourself running down the hall to make it to a bathroom in time, then catching your breath as you lock yourself in your classroom for the last two minutes of the break, sobbing at your desk. You may believe that your students need you so much that you can't possibly call a substitute teacher. You may not want to *waste* a maternity-leave day on sick leave. You may believe that you have to be strong and stoic and push through in order to be respected by your colleagues and administration. However, what you honestly *need* is to take care of your body. Additionally, what your students likely need is a healthy, responsive teacher. So, you call in a substitute teacher.

We need to be able to give ourselves the gift of reflection and time to make space to take the next best steps forward (Neff, 2011). Mindfulness is an important foundation for creating a reframe mindset. It allows us to tune in and become familiar with what we need most to replenish ourselves.

Propel Yourself Forward

Crafting an empowering narrative about your struggle is one part of the journey to post-traumatic growth. So much of true transformation comes from our subsequent action (Meichenbaum, 2006).

Anchoring yourself to incremental, predictable, and routinized behaviors that enable forward motion is not only healthy but contributes to resilience. For Janelle Morrison (page 42), the incremental actions she took every day contributed to her recovery. Her dedication to her goal was non-negotiable; she took consistent action every single day for two whole years. For Allie Apels (page 39), dreaming up a solution to the challenging behaviors in her kindergarten class through the Kindness Ninjas movement created the ideal momentum to foster positive action. Sometimes we need to counter the effects of empathic distress by keeping our *purpose* in mind as the educator of a traumatized child. At times, we need to take time away from the classroom to recover when we are not feeling well. What are you going to do now? What (micro)action can you take to propel yourself forward?

Anyone can become intentional in creating a powerful path forward; we simply need to believe that it is within our power to do so and set ourselves up for resiliency success.

How to Practice Self-Regulation

Part of what contributes to burnout is the stress cycle and our inability to manage the effects of external stress on our moods and bodies (Shanker, 2017). While much of our external stress is beyond our control, psychologist Stuart Shanker (2017) suggests taking inventory of the stressors in your life, identifying the ones within your control, and actively working to reduce these ones to help you to be more self-regulated and resilient on a day-to-day basis.

Self-regulation is the process by which our bodies and minds constantly seek equilibrium. The stressors in our lives directly impact our self-regulation and, therefore, our resiliency. See table 2.2 (page 54) for examples of our four dominant energetic states or moods, often affected by our environmental and internal stressors.

TABLE 2.2: FOUR DOMINANT ENERGETIC MOODS OR STATES

Tension	**Low-energy, high-tension state** Negative affect The individual is: • Sad • Restless • Bored	**High-energy, high-tension state** Negative affect The individual is: • Angry • Anxious
	Low-energy, low-tension state Positive affect The individual is: • Relaxed • Calm	**High-energy, low-tension state** Ideal state; positive affect The individual is: • Happy • Excited

Energy

Source: Adapted from Shanker, 2017; Thayer, 1996.

Shanker identifies five types of stressors that can affect our mental state, including physical stress, emotional stress, cognitive stress, social stress, and pro-social stress.

1. **Physical stress:** Noise, lights, pain, and even the proximity of other people can cause undue stress on your nervous system. Recall the COVID-19 pandemic of 2020. For many educators who had to teach face-to-face in school buildings, it was often stressful to be in the classroom near other people because we were so attuned to the possibility of unknowingly becoming infected and because we had very little control over our physical stress.

2. **Emotional stress:** Strong emotions (positive and negative) can be overwhelming and even scary, so some of our behavior comes from shutting down when the emotions become too big to handle. For example, when students in my first-grade class are in an elevated conflict, I often feel a rising tension and alertness within myself. Positive emotions can be hard, too. Any special holiday can be challenging in the classroom because the children are so excited, which can elevate emotional stress even though it is a positive event.

3. **Cognitive stress:** A stress that makes a big demand on the working memory in our brain can be categorized as cognitive stress. For example, we might have a low frustration tolerance when we are learning something new that is cognitively demanding, like a new app or technology for classroom learning.

4. **Social stress:** Social stress can be challenging because it revolves around the topic of belonging, which is one of our fundamental emotional needs (see chapter 1, page 11). For example, a new teacher could experience social stress while trying to fit in with colleagues, managing disagreements and differences of opinions, and even making small talk at a holiday party.

5. **Pro-social stress:** Our own ability to tune into the stress of others can be stressful. Empathy can cause us stress. Navigating parent communication can be challenging when there is a conflict or if a parent is distressed, for instance. Effective communication requires that we use our empathy skills to take others' perspectives, which can cause pro-social stress. Many of us seek to please, at any cost, and sometimes this means that we want to *fix* any miscommunications that occur. When we find ourselves trying to people please by mind reading, or when we consistently find ourselves managing others' strong emotions, we can feel emotionally burnt out. It is possible to reduce the pro-social stress. Decreasing life's negative stressors, Shanker (2017) asserts, can have a positive effect on your well-being and mood.

Table 2.3 (page 56) provides a breakdown of these five stress domains and corresponding examples for decreasing them.

When we encounter hardship, resilience is the ability to get back up, dust ourselves off, and perhaps even embrace a richer, more dynamic version of our lives. The key to resilience lies in our ability to examine our beliefs and the story we tell about our challenges, to commit to reframing the negative beliefs, and to set ourselves up for success by taking action upon that which we *can* control. By actively decreasing the stressors within our lives, we dedicate ourselves to a new way forward. Avoiding adversity is impossible. However, we can learn to adapt and grow into ourselves as we bounce forward through hard times. We can develop a reframe mindset that encourages us to face any obstacles within our path.

TABLE 2.3: THE FIVE STRESS DOMAINS

Domain	Example Ways to Minimize Stressors
Physical Stress	• Decrease noise. • Turn off lights. • Go outside for fresh air. • Listen to calming music. • Nourish yourself (eat healthily and drink water).
Emotional Stress	• Build in some reflection time (see chapter 1, page 19). • Take a few deep breaths. • Reduce the number of things you need to do. • Refer to your self-care action list (see page 31). • Name your feelings.
Cognitive Stress	• Give yourself more time to do tasks that are difficult. • Outsource tasks that add to your cognitive load (for example, use services like Teachers Pay Teachers to get you started on planning big units or outsource filing your taxes). • Dedicate uninterrupted blocks of time for tricky tasks (multitasking doesn't always work). • Write out your to-do list so that you don't have to worry about forgetting.
Social Stress	• Seek out quality social time with friends and family. • Avoid situations that call for small talk. • Give yourself some recharge time or alone time when you are overwhelmed by people. • Cancel plans if you're not feeling up to socializing.
Pro-social Stress	• Allow yourself permission to create healthy boundaries for yourself. • If a situation puts you into empathetic distress (see page 15), it's okay to take a break from the situation and ask for help from a professional. • Turn off the news and social media. • Put yourself first, in spite of guilt you might be feeling.

Source: Adapted from Shanker, 2017.

Strategies to Ignite Your Reframing Fire

This section of the chapter includes strategies that will strengthen your resiliency. Through positively reframing thoughts, inner self-talk, and beliefs, we can change the way we show up for others and for ourselves.

Reframing Strategies

In this section, you begin with a journaling exercise that encourages you to examine a situation that is particularly challenging and find a way forward through specific reflective questioning. Next, you will explore the power of positive mantras using a framework that encourages you to imagine a more positive self-talk script. Finally, you will end this section with a letter to yourself, through which you will reflect on the strengths you bring to your role as a teacher, celebrate the highlights of your school year, think about some of the powerful lessons you've learned, and reimagine the way in which you have had a positive impact on those around you.

Resiliency Journaling Exercise

When you're dealing with a difficult event or situation in your life, it can be helpful to observe your thoughts and beliefs about it, to identify and accept what is out of your control, to alter what is within your control, and to reframe the situation in such a way that you can see the opportunity for growth within it. This exercise helps you do this.

1. Think of a challenge in your life right now that is heavy on your heart.

2. In a journal or your phone, summarize your challenge using one or two sentences.

3. Refer to the "Resiliency Journaling Exercise" reproducible (page 62) and follow the remainder of the prompts.

While reframing is a process, journaling will enable you to practice the process until it feels second nature. Don't forget to exercise some of the core elements of self-compassion from chapter 1 (page 22) as you journal. Be kind to yourself!

Positive Mantras Exercise

Mantras are short phrases or affirmations that have roots in Buddhism and are often thought to have powerful influence on people's well-being by inducing a calm mental state (Lynch et al., 2018). In fact, researchers are starting to find that mantras have the capacity to quiet the negative internal default chatter or self-talk within your mind (Lynch et al., 2018). Positive mantras or affirmations can become a script for positive self-talk that can counteract your limiting beliefs about yourself (Seligman, 2011). Positive self-talk is an essential component of cultivating an optimistic outlook and resilient mindset, which are keys to reframing your mindset and warding off burnout (Maslach & Leiter, 2016). Try the following four-step exercise.

1. Make a list of three character qualities you consider weaknesses or negative beliefs you have about your efficacy, professionally or personally. Write them into a sentence in the first person, present tense (for example, *I am always late. I always procrastinate. I am selfish when I do things for myself. I am too serious. I can't learn new things. I'm terrible at technology*).

2. For each of these negative qualities or beliefs, think of a reframe that could cast the weakness as a strength. For example, if you believe laziness is a weakness of yours, it could also mean that you're able to relax and take care of yourself. If you think you're too serious, it could mean that you are dependable and professional. If you don't think you're good at learning new technology, it could mean that you have identified a new area of growth.

3. Once you think of a reframe for every corresponding weakness, write the reframes down in the first person, present tense (for example, *It is healthy to relax and take care of myself. I am dependable and professional at work. I can work hard to learn new things*). See table 2.4 for additional examples.

4. Keep these reframes tucked in your journal or display them more prominently on sticky notes on your mirror or fridge, as a screensaver on your computer monitor at work, or even as an hourly prompt in your phone as a daily reminder of the importance of reframing your negative self-talk.

TABLE 2.4: EXAMPLES OF REFRAMING NEGATIVE SELF-TALK AS POSITIVE MANTRAS

Negative Self-Talk	Positive Mantra
Nothing ever goes my way! My lessons always seem to fall flat with students.	There is always something for which to be grateful, even in the challenges.
I'm not a fun teacher.	I am a calm and grounded role model for my students.
Teaching makes me so busy; I can't catch my breath!	I am in control of my choices as an educator.
I am no good at this tech stuff! My students are missing out because of me!	I don't know how to do it, yet, but I can learn if I just take it slow and steady.
I am so worried about how hard this school year will be.	This school year, I just have to take the next best step.
I don't have time for self-care! I need to spend my time on prepping for school.	My students will be better off if I make myself a priority.

Motivational Mantras

David Jay, aka The Dope Educator, teaches in Memphis, Tennessee. He greets every one of his seventy students with a personalized handshake every day and incorporates mantras into his day as a means of helping them to rise to their potential (Michael, 2019f).

One of the ways he ends his classes is to gather his students in a circle and sing along to the song "Hall of Fame" by The Script (2012).

In my own classroom, I stenciled four big inspiring phrases on the wall to greet everyone who enters my classroom.

You Are So Loved

Welcome

Be Kind to Yourself

Start Each Day With a Grateful Heart

Incorporating mantras into your classroom routine is a powerful way to help students to program their minds with positive self-talk.

Letter to Yourself Exercise

At the end of one school year several years ago, in the busy month of June, I started the practice of writing a letter to myself. Like a ritual, I would seal the letter and place it in the left-hand drawer of my desk on the last day of school. At the end of September, during the beginning of the following school year, I would open the letter and read each word slowly, with intention, allowing the message to sink into my skeptical spirit, reminding myself that, yes, these students would get to where they needed to go—I just had to meet them where they were. Patience, time, and faith were all I needed to keep in my mind over the coming months to stay afloat and avoid burning out.

The magic of the learning and deep growth that occurs within each child seems nearly impossible to a teacher's mind at the beginning of the year. And so, the letter served to remind my September self that according to my June self it would all work out.

No matter how long you've been teaching, the beginning of the year can seem overwhelming, so I urge you to write, as in the following four-step exercise, a gift of insight and wisdom to yourself at the end of every year.

1. Start with some paper, an envelope, and a pen. Since writing this letter is such a symbolic act of self-care, why not splurge on some special stationery and pen?

2. Reflect on where you find yourself in this moment, at the end of a full school year. Choose any combination of questions from the "Letter to Yourself Questions" reproducible (page 63) and answer them using a few phrases within the letter to yourself. Write it as though you are writing to a friend, reminding him or her of all that went well, all that he or she learned, and recognizing the challenges he or she overcame.

3. Sign the letter, seal it in the envelope, and address the letter to yourself. Keep it in a conspicuous place where you'll be sure to find it at the beginning of the year or mail the letter to yourself.

4. Set a reminder in your phone or on your calendar to open the letter in the third week of school, once the shininess of *new beginnings* has worn off and the overwhelm starts to creep in. Your words will likely remind you how capable and competent you are. It will inspire you to breathe deeply and accept the uncertainty of the year ahead.

Conclusion

Resilience is an essential key to becoming wholehearted educators, since teaching can be exhausting and stressful, and even trigger trauma responses within us. Being able to take our experiences, process them, and create helpful internal narratives enables us to reframe our circumstances in positive ways so that we have more to offer our students, colleagues, school community, and our loved ones.

In chapter 2, we learned about the research related to resiliency and how to cultivate a reframe mindset. We explored the challenges of restrictive personal beliefs and how to reprogram our thoughts when we feel limited by our own narratives through resiliency journaling, crafting positive mantras for our internal self-talk, learning to actively reduce the stressors in our life, and reminding ourselves of our capacity for resiliency through the letter to ourselves.

Resiliency Journaling Exercise

Goal	Journal Prompt
Identify the hardest part of the challenge.	*The hardest part for me is* _____
Identify your feelings.	*I am feeling* _____
Name your beliefs and thoughts, then identify if they are helpful or hurtful.	*My thinking is* _____ *I believe that* _____ *Are these thoughts and beliefs helpful or hurtful?*
Make a list of factors that are out of your control.	*These factors are out of my control:*
Make a list of factors that are within your control.	*These factors are within my control:*
Identify the learning within the challenge.	*How can I best interpret this situation?*
Imagine an ideal outcome.	*What is the best possible outcome within this situation?*
Make an action plan.	*What small action could I take to move me forward in this challenge that is within my locus of control?*

Letter to Yourself Questions

Please answer the following questions and reflect.

- What went well this year?

- What was a challenge I overcame?

- What was something I learned from the students?

- What was something I learned from the parents?

- What was something I learned from my colleagues?

- What was my proudest moment this year?

- What was something that surprised me at school this year?

- What was my biggest perceived failure? What did I learn?

Page 1 of 2

- What personal habits helped me to be successful this year?

- What organizational systems helped me do my job?

- Who helped me to feel most connected to my school this year?

- What are some professional and personal goals I crushed this year?

- What is something new I tried that worked well?

- What is the one thing I need to remember about myself as I start this journey with a new class?

- What do I need to remind myself as I commence a new year?

- What piece of advice could I have used last year that would have made things easier?

REFOCUS

How to Harness Intentionality to Reach Your Goals and Dreams

A goal without a plan is just a wish.

—Antoine de Saint-Exupéry

Feeling burnt out in education can fuel a lack of purpose and direction that can leave teachers feeling restless, frustrated, and even down on themselves (Kaschka, Korczak, & Broich, 2011). Part of being resilient in the face of adversity and stressful times is directly impacted by our sense of forward motion, our ability to create a plan of action related to specific, meaningful goals we set for ourselves personally and professionally as educators. In order to feel wholehearted in our role as educators, we can refocus ourselves toward goals that align with who we are and where we want to be in our classrooms and in our personal lives (Santoro, 2018). It is helpful to consider our values, ideals, and motivations to calibrate our inner compass so that we can find purpose and meaning in our job as educators (Lavy & Bocker, 2017).

In this chapter, you will explore what the research says about refocusing on appropriate goals. You will learn about types of goals, their purpose, and the benefits of setting and achieving goals within an educational context. You will discover the nine steps of goal setting and learn the SMART goals framework before delving into the neuroscience behind goal setting. In the second half of this chapter, you'll discover several strategies to improve your ability to refocus and set goals, including strategies for identifying your personal vision, navigating timing and scheduling issues, and finding ways to keep your personal fires burning.

What the Research Says About Refocusing

Educators who tend to feel deeply connected to the broader purpose of their role in schools as difference-makers often tend to be happier, more fulfilled, and less stressed out (Malin, 2018). Goal setting is one of the best ways that individuals can connect with that inner sense of purpose and passion, which results in an overall sense of efficacy and contentment (Hooker, 2020). As Viktor Frankl (1984) said in his book *Man's Search for Meaning*, "What [people] actually need is not a tensionless state but rather the striving and struggling for some goal worthy of [them]. What [we] need is not the discharge of tension at any cost, but the call of a potential meaning waiting to be fulfilled by [us]" (p. 166). Our human need to create meaning is one of the primary motivations in life. The meaning of life comes from our roles, goals, and achievements within it.

Kindergarten Kindnesses

Laurie McIntosh (@mrsmacskinders) is a kindergarten teacher in Alberta, Canada. She has made it her purpose to teach her students about kindness and share her inspiring ideas with her growing online community through social media (Michael, 2019e). The following ideas have worked well with her classes.

- **Kindness capes:** Laurie encourages her kindergarteners to think of kindness as a superpower. On special days, she puts individual capes on each of her students' seats to signal that they will be doing something kind as a class. She and her class often visit senior centers, spread kindness through community parades, raise awareness about homelessness through fundraising, and more.

- **DNA inventory:** Every year, Laurie does a Dreams, Needs, and Abilities (DNA) Inventory of her students, helping all see their potential, the areas they need to grow, and the strengths they already possess. Much of her teaching around kindness starts with encouraging the students to love themselves.

- **The Kind Club (@The_Kind_Club):** Laurie launched the international kindness group The Kind Club with a fellow teacher to promote kindness across the world through monthly challenges that are

accessible on twitter and through their website (https://sites.google
.com/view/thekindclub/home). Some of my favorite challenges include
making kindness bookmarks for the local library, painting rocks with
inspirational messages to hide within the community, and doing a daily
gratitude challenge with your class.

Laurie's focus on kindness has led her to make some powerful connections
with world-renowned educators, authors, and entertainers, and has landed
her on *The Ellen DeGeneres Show* twice! She even wrote a book with Jody
Carrington, *Teachers These Days*, that shares her ideas with educators.

Laurie is an example of an educator who leads with purpose and who
consistently sets meaningful goals for her practice. She works hard every
day to infuse a magical love of learning for her students and, in turn, feels
filled up herself.

Self-management and responsible decision making are essential components that
contribute to educator well-being, confidence, and social-emotional competence
(Oberle & Schonert-Reichl, 2016; Vesely, Saklofske, & Leschied, 2013). According
to leading educator and well-being researcher Kimberly Schonert-Reichl (2017),
"Teaching is one of the most stressful occupations; moreover, stress in the classroom is contagious—simply put, stressed-out teachers tend to have stressed-out
students" (p.137). Feeling contentment and passion about our role as teachers is a
key indicator of wellness, whereas lack of efficacy, cynicism, and exhaustion point
to potential burnout (Oberle & Schonert-Reichl, 2016). Educators who demonstrate the following traits tend to be more successful in hitting their personal and
professional targets.

1. Effective goal-setting habits

2. The self-discipline to acknowledge one's feelings and control one's
   impulses to overcome inevitable distractions and mishaps along the
   journey of achieving goals

3. The self-motivation to keep working toward important goals

4. The organization capability to manage one's time, physical space,
   materials, and information in pursuit of those goals (Brunsting,
   Sreckovic, & Lane, 2014)

When we are able to successfully and consistently meet our own professional and
personal goals with a heart-centered approach, it's more likely we'll feel successful
and happy not only in our classrooms but in our lives (Kunter & Holzberger, 2014).

Goal Setting and the Elastic Band Analogy

When addressing goals, I like to use the elastic band analogy that I learned once in conversation with my friend, Kristin Weins (@kwiens62), an inclusion coach in the Sooke School District in British Columbia. Imagine that we are always in forward motion, holding onto an elastic band that is attached to our future goal. As we move toward our goals, the elastic band may swing from the right to the left, advance closer to the goal, or seemingly stretch farther from it. If you pull the band too tightly too quickly, the elastic band snaps; the goal is unachievable when it is unrealistic or too lofty. An unrealistic goal can cause immense stress, disappointment, and loss of self-confidence. Conversely, if the elastic band is too loose, the goal is not challenging enough and does not stretch us into a positive and ideal learning zone, a place where we can experience positive transformation and growth. Instead, we can find ourselves stuck in the status quo, unable to grow and push ourselves beyond our current experience. An elastic band with no tension cannot perform its stretchy function as an elastic band. Goals need to have enough tension to become the catalyst for positive growth but not be so tight that they become unachievable. What matters most is that we refocus and attach our elastic to an optimistic goal for the future and that no matter how much we seemingly deviate from the path toward it, we can trust that the elastic will stay in place, pulling us and gently guiding us to the future place we wish and envision ourselves to be (K. Weins, personal communication, February 8, 2021).

When it comes to leading a life of purpose, intention, and meaning, setting goals is essential. Goals are the target for our own competence and performance, and they represent a consistent approach to taking action, assessing that action for efficacy, and calibrating ourselves toward an overall positive vision for ourselves. Goal setting is the process through which we go about achieving our targets. According to researchers Edwin Locke and Gary Latham (2019), who spent many years researching the theory of goal setting, a life without goals is an existence devoid of meaning. We can't remain passive if we want to thrive as educators. To thrive in and out of the classroom, all of us need goals and plans of action to propel us into the lives we wish to lead (Kunter & Holzberger, 2014).

Types of Goals

There are two main goal types that have been identified, according to researchers, performance and mastery goals (Darnon, Butera, & Harackiewicz, 2007).

Performance goals tend to be aligned to external locus of success, while mastery goals are related to an intrinsic sense of achievement and success.

1. **Performance goals:** The most straightforward type of goal is a *performance goal* (Janke et al., 2016). There is usually a finite beginning and end that defines the target, such that it is easy to declare our success or failure. Additionally, performance goals tend to be connected to external indicators of success, meaning that we rely on the judgement of others to determine our ultimate success or failure.

   When it comes to teaching, we co-create, on a macro scale, many performance goals (large and small) for our students throughout the year, and every single day we do so at the micro level. For example, we set goals for our students related to specific independent reading levels by the end of term, or goals connected to their ability to learn the multiplication tables by the end of an arbitrary two-week period and demonstrate their understanding by getting 10 out of 10 on the quiz.

   Since performance goals are based on a finite, external outcome, it can be challenging to stay motivated to continue pursuing the goal once we've hit a specific target (Janke et al., 2016). Similarly, our motivation tends to decrease if we struggle to achieve the goal; we can become overwhelmed or discouraged by the lack of tangible progress. Moreover, performance goals are rooted in scarcity, the belief that there is only so much of the proverbial pie to go around, which can fuel an unhealthy sense of competition and a desire to win at all costs.

2. **Mastery goals:** Alternatively, mastery goals are about process and gaining a sense of mastery over a skill or approach (Poortvliet & Darnon, 2013). Mastery goals relate to internal indicators of success in a particular task or area, not external success markers (Schiefele & Schaffner, 2015). When we set mastery goals for ourselves, we aim to become the best we can be. We run our own race, and we don't compare our achievements to those of others. Mastery goals don't tend to have a clear end point, so maintaining motivation is about longevity and stamina as well as nurturing the belief that incremental improvement is the marker of success. Essentially, there is always something more to strive for. The challenging aspect of mastery goals is that they are more fluid, less finite, and more difficult to measure (Poortvliet & Darnon, 2013). A more abundant approach to goal

setting, however, enables us to strive toward our potential, meeting our ambitions at our own pace.

In the classroom, we can set mastery goals around skill acquisition and application. For example, we could set the goal for a student to use grade-level texts to gain an understanding of a specific topic during a unit in social studies. Another example might be encouraging a child to apply a specific problem-solving approach on the playground by the end of term.

The Purpose of Goals

People often feel the need to plan for the future. Thus, we create goals for ourselves for two main reasons: problem solving or inspired visioning (Chowdhury, 2020).

1. **Problem-solving goal setting:** The first reason for creating goals comes from a place of deficiency. We assess our lives, personally or professionally, and come to the realization that something needs to change because the current status quo is no longer serving us. We see a problem, and we want to solve it (McDaniel, 2016). Those who seek to improve deficiencies in their lives tend to be problem solvers. Problem solvers are rooted in the present circumstances and tend to be detail oriented. They want to anticipate pitfalls and maintain a steady grasp on reality as they work to improve their current lived situation. Problem solvers tend to be results based, routine oriented, and risk averse.

2. **Inspired goal setting:** The second impetus for goal setting comes from an inspired vision for a positive future (McDaniel, 2016). In other words, instead of seeing what isn't working, we find ourselves aligning our intentions for a possible and optimistic future. Inspired goal setters envision future possibilities and the big picture. Inspired goal setters look toward the future with a positive, passionate, and often ambitious (perhaps, even unrealistic) outlook about what could be. Goal setters enjoy innovation, creativity, and uncertainty.

Identifying the type of goal setter you are helps to align you with a clearer vision of what you want for your future (McDaniel, 2016). Next, let's look at some of the relevant benefits of goal setting within the education setting.

The Benefits of Goal Setting in Education

When it comes to education, teachers who set goals for themselves often see marked improvements in their classrooms and self-efficacy (Paulick, Retelsdorf, & Möller, 2013). Educators who specifically work to improve their teaching abilities tend to report an increased passion for teaching, believe they are better teachers overall, and identify a more positive self-concept (Camp, 2017).

Setting goals can also improve the relationship we have with our students as well as their achievement in the classroom (Butler & Shibaz, 2014). For instance, when educators set relationship goals with their students, the students tend to identify that their teacher is part of their support network, and their motivation increases (Butler, 2012; Schiefele & Schaffner, 2015). Furthermore, goal setting can be particularly important for educators who are just starting out in their careers (Paulick et al., 2013). Goals can help us establish what kind of educator we wish to be and strive toward that ideal (Mansfield & Beltman, 2014). Moreover, we can look back on a year of growth with pride as we celebrate our accomplishments.

Undoubtedly, goal setting is an essential part of our personal and professional growth as educators, but it is also an important part of our students' development (Moeller, Theiler, & Wu, 2011). Figuring out our goals is only part of the equation. What's truly important is recognizing the essential components for creating powerful, effective goals that will help kindle your professional and personal improvement throughout the next school year (O'Brien, Pearpoint, & Kahn, 2015).

How to Formulate Goals

While it can be easy for some of us educators to create clear goals, for others the process of trying to figure out our end point can seem impossible to identify. Whether you are a problem-solving goal setter or an inspired one, creating a clear road map isn't always easy. Whether you tend to look at things from the zoomed-out big picture to the zoomed-in small parts, or if you tend to see processes more from a small-parts to big-picture perspective, there are some basic and essential components to creating goals that have been found to be effective, no matter the circumstance. The following nine actions offer an effective and proven approach to formulating goals (O'Brien et al., 2015).

1. Get Clear

Often, we struggle to create and achieve goals because we are too vague and broad in our approach. It's helpful to get clear and focus specifically on your purpose (Locke & Latham, 2002; Morisano, Hirsh, Peterson, Pihl, & Shore, 2010). Here are some clarifying questions that can support you in tuning into your overall purpose, personally as an individual and professionally as an educator.

- What is most important in your life?
- What gives meaning to what you do in the classroom?
- What helps guide you when you feel lost?
- What keeps you going when things are challenging?
- What are some key turning points that inform your decision to move forward differently?
- What inspires you?
- Who are some people who professionally and personally inspire you to be the best version of yourself?

2. Visualize

Our imaginations are a rich resource when it comes to creating a positive vision for our future. According to research, visualization is a strong motivator to pursue and achieve our goals (Cheema & Bagchi, 2011). When we are able to see ourselves having already completed a task or achievement, we feel more motivated to continue our pursuit of that goal because it seems to be within our grasp (Cheema & Bagchi, 2011). Often, all that we need to do is give ourselves some clear prompts, time, and the ability to get lost in the possibility of *what could be*. Using your senses to anchor a future vision enables you to create a path forward.

- What does success look like in the classroom or your personal life?
- What does success in your professional or personal life feel like?
- What are some of the experiences you have when things are going well in your professional and personal life? (Think about this through the senses—consider taste, smell, and touch.)

3. Identify Your Current Story

An important step in creating a new path forward through goal setting and intentional actions starts with acknowledging and naming your current reality. Often there is a gap between where you are in the current moment and the place you wish to be (MindTools, n.d.b.). It can be tough for you to align yourself to a new future if you haven't identified the distance between your goals and your current reality. Realizing some of the difficult realities you might have to overcome helps to render a goal more realistic.

- What are three main elements of your future vision for yourself professionally (in the classroom) and personally (in your life)?

- What are three aspects of your life that are currently different than that vision?

- What will likely be the easiest shifts for you as you move forward toward your new goals?

4. Identify Your Gifts

An important aspect of setting professional (classroom) and personal (life) goals is understanding the skills and strengths you specifically bring to the table, based on your tendencies and past experiences (Bouskila-Yam & Kluger, 2011). Capitalizing on these strengths not only builds momentum and endurance as you journey toward your vision but also enables you to approach tasks with a deep belief in your own efficacy.

- When you are at your best, what are the strengths you tend to bring to others professionally and personally?

- What makes you feel most satisfied when you are working with others in the classroom and within your life?

- What tends to bring out your best capabilities?

- What are some of your strengths, according to other people (your colleagues, administrators, educational assistants, and even students)?

5. Recognize the Roadblocks

Anticipating some of the challenges ahead is an important component of goal setting (O'Brien et al., 2015). Being blindsided by unexpected hiccups or resource deficiencies can be crippling in your quest to achieve your goals. Forward thinking is an important part of being successful and gaining a sense of self-efficacy. Trying to identify potential difficulties can set you up for long-term success, even if there are some bumps in the road. As you set forth to achieve a new goal, ask yourself the following questions.

- What do you anticipate might be the hardest challenge as you move forward in achieving your goals?

- What are some ways you can plan ahead to avoid these challenges?

- What are some of the connections you need to make to achieve this goal?

- What are some of the resources you need to overcome some of the roadblocks you encounter?

- What are some of the things you need to learn in order to achieve this goal?

- What might you need to stop in order to achieve your goal?

6. Identify Partners and Allies

Setting and achieving goals may seem like an independent endeavor; however, research has shown that the more you involve and invite others into your goal-setting journey, the more successful you will be in achieving the goals you set for yourself (O'Brien et al., 2015). When people are invested in your successes, there is a potential for them to contribute their strengths to your mission. Additional resources are a welcome contribution to achieving your goals. Take some time to reflect on the following questions.

- Who can help you with your goal?

- How can this person help you?

- Is there a mutual benefit to your collaboration?

- What are some of the connections you need to foster to achieve your goal?

- Who might act as an accountability support or a coach?

7. Select an Action Strategy

Now that you've established a clear vision, identified your strengths and the roadblocks related to a goal, and highlighted some of the important people who will help you realize your ambitions, it's important to take action. Action planning ensures that your goals transform from idealized wishes to tangible results (O'Brien et al., 2015). Action planning requires that you examine the goals and your current story as well as your strengths and limitations to craft a clear, step-by-step approach to achievement. Action planning involves identifying the big steps you need to take to craft your desired future.

- What are the major milestones and big steps you need to take to achieve your vision? What do you need? Who can help you stay accountable? What are the timelines within which you would like to achieve the bigger goal and corresponding milestones? How will you know when the big steps are achieved? How will you check your progress?

- What are some of the smaller action steps within each of these bigger milestones? What will you need to achieve these smaller goals? Who will help you remain accountable to the smaller steps? What are the timelines within which you would like to achieve the smaller action steps? How will you identify when the smaller action steps are completed? How will you consistently check progress?

8. Commit

It's one thing to have a vision and create a plan, but at some point you have to level with yourself and consider whether or not you realistically have the ability to commit to the pursuit of the goal. Often, educators have no problem taking on new commitments. The tough part, however, can stem from the need to curate and reduce our commitments (O'Brien et al., 2015). We can do just about anything, but we can't do everything! To be effective, you have to choose your commitments with intentionality. You must simplify your pursuits to amplify your outcomes.

- Are you willing to commit to this professional or personal journey?

- What commitments can you consistently make to yourself and others to make this goal happen?

- What might you have to drop professionally or personally to take on this new commitment?

9. Overcome Obstacles

While you might have effectively considered relevant roadblocks and limited resources, when it comes to goals, there is always the potential of being caught off-guard by events or circumstances beyond your control (O'Brien et al., 2015). Blind spots are also hard to guard against, so you must be prepared to confront and accept obstacles as they arise. Part of being adaptable requires you to call on your reflective capabilities. Planning for regular check-ins related to your progress toward a goal is an important part of assessing whether you are on the right track or whether you need to refocus your efforts. Making time for reflection and problem solving is important. See chapter 1 (page 11) for strategies and approaches for carving time out of your busy day and consider the following questions.

- What is working well?

- What is not working so well?

- What have you learned so far? What do you need to do differently?

- Is your broader goal still aligned with who you are, what you need, and where you'd like to go?

- Are there any problems with your current trajectory? What are some of the most pressing issues related to your goal? What are some alternative ways that you could get around or solve this issue? What is the best solution you could adopt moving forward toward your bigger goal?

There are so many specific approaches to goal setting that work well. Essentially, however you address them, successful goals require you to get clear about and visualize the outcome, address your current circumstances, identify strengths and road-blocks, identify your social connections who will help you move forward toward your goals, develop action plans, commit wholeheartedly to your forward motion, and address issues as they arise. Being aware and considering goal setting within this broader framework enables you to be more successful in your endeavors.

The SMART Goals Framework

Once you have a clear sense of the areas in which you would like to make a change, you need to get even more specific to bring your goals to life. Many people in the field of education rely on the SMART goals framework to set goals alongside students and colleagues, which has been shown through extensive research to be an effective goal-setting framework due to its specificity and intentionality (see, for example, Haughey, 2014; Kleingeld, van Mierlo, & Arends, 2011).

First coined in 1981 by businessman George T. Doran, the SMART goals frame-work has since evolved to describe an effective checklist that comprises the import-ant qualities of a goal (Haughey, 2014; Rubin, 2002). The SMART framework states that effective goals must be specific, measurable, attainable, relevant, and time-bound (Haughey, 2014; MindTools, n.d.c. While there are different versions of the acronym, including additional letters *E* (evaluate) and *R* (review), the version I've referenced is useful and widely used in education and business institutions throughout the globe (Rubin, 2002). Figure 3.1 contains detailed explanations and examples of the SMART goals framework.

Step	Questions to Ask Yourself	Description	Examples
Specific	• What do I want to achieve? • Why is this goal important? • Who will be involved? • Where will it take place? • Which resources will I need?	Specify the action to be taken, including when it will happen, where it will take place, who will participate, and what will be involved.	Instead of saying, "I will be more engaging at school," say, "I will increase student engagement in my classroom discussions this week by introducing a new provocation each day to spark interest and dialogue."
Measurable	• How often? • How many? • How will I know when I've achieved my goal?	Specify how you will measure your progress on the goal. Keeping measurable goals helps us maintain our motivation and track our progress.	Instead of saying, "I will conference more frequently with my students," say, "I will dedicate three blocks per week to conferencing with each of the students in my class."
Attainable	• What will I need to succeed? • Within the context of the realistic constraints, is this goal doable?	Specify, using the *elastic band analogy*, how you will make this goal achievable but also a bit of a stretch. If we are stretching ourselves or our resources beyond the realistic boundaries, it can be difficult to achieve the goal.	Instead of saying, "I will finish my master's, teach full-time, start a new business, and raise my twin toddlers this year," it might be more helpful to focus on one or two big goals like "This year I will focus on teaching full-time, take one course per semester toward my master's, and raise my toddlers."

Figure 3.1: SMART goals framework.

continued →

Step	Questions to Ask Yourself	Description	Examples
Relevant	• Does this goal matter to me? • Is this the right time for this goal? • Am I the right person for this? • Does this match my vision for the future?	Keep goals relevant. This ensures that they align with our values and vision for ourselves, making it more likely for us to achieve them.	Instead of saying, "I am feeling overwhelmed by the demands of my spouse's new job, my current role in the classroom, and my parental obligations, but I'll take on the new role as department head since I don't want to disappoint my principal," it might be better to say, "I want to advance my career, but this is not the right year for me to accept the department head role."
Time-Bound	• When will I start? • When does it need to be completed? • What are my short-term obligations? • What are my long-term obligations? • What can I start on, today?	Recognize that timing is an important part of efficacy when it comes to creating goals that work. Part of guarding against overwhelm and procrastination relates setting realistic timelines for task completion.	Instead of saying, "One day, I'll organize my teaching binders and dedicate myself to a more linear approach to lesson planning," you might say, "I'd like to organize my teaching binders, so I am going to start by organizing one binder every Monday during my prep block, which gives me a six-week timeline to complete the overall task of organizing my classroom materials."

The Psychology of Goal Setting

While it would be wonderful if we could simply attain success in achieving our goals simply by following the refocusing frameworks proven to work, unfortunately for most of us in education, there are additional variables that can make goal setting and achievement especially challenging. First, we need to consider the ways in which we approach inner and outer expectations, since goals are expectations placed upon the trajectory of our future. Next, it's helpful to examine the nature of our goals and whether intrinsic or extrinsic motivators will enable us to reach our aspirations more effectively (just like we would with the students in our classrooms). Finally, it can be eye-opening to explore some of the brain circuitry that lends itself to certain goals but thwarts others, as neuroscience provides insight into some of the goals that might be harder to achieve than others.

One of the challenges many educators face every day is determining how to motivate people, including themselves, to reach their goals. Gretchen Rubin's (2017) Four Tendencies framework reveals how people respond to internal and external, or *outer*, expectations, which can provide insight into how we can be more successful in reaching our objectives and helping those around us to reach theirs.

According to Rubin (2017), all of us face two types of expectations: (1) outer expectations, such as the expectation to meet curricular outcomes within a particular time frame or to meet the demands of a challenging parent working to meet his or her child's needs; and (2) inner expectations, such as the goal to create deeper connections with students or to begin packing ourselves healthier lunch meals for school. How we react to the inner and outer expectations indicates our tendency profile from one of Rubin's Four Tendencies. When we understand our own tendency, we are more likely to work with our strengths to increase the likelihood of hitting a personal target. When we understand the tendencies of our students, it's more likely we can help them reach their potential in the classroom.

In her book, *The Four Tendencies*, Rubin (2017) outlines how people with each of the Four Tendencies respond to expectations in different ways.

1. **Upholder tendency:** Upholders tend to meet outer expectations with ease and are also successful in meeting internal expectations. For instance, Jane may be so dedicated to submitting her report cards on time that she'll work on them every evening for several hours until they are complete, and when it comes to committing to her goal of drinking eight glasses of water per day at school, she consistently meets her target. Upholders tend to have no problem refocusing and meeting their own personal and professional goals. Often, since upholders tend to devote themselves to routines, they can struggle or tighten when things are out of their control. For example, someone like Jane may struggle to adapt to a new curriculum at first because of unclear expectations. Upholders often benefit from learning to go with the flow.

2. **Obliger tendency:** Obligers tend to meet outer expectations but struggle with their own inner expectations. Obligers often tend to be people pleasers, often putting others' needs and expectations before their own. For example, Tim will volunteer to stay late to coach practice every single day after school because it's a good thing for students, but he can't bring himself to go to the gym and exercise regularly for his own health. Since obligers do well with outer accountability, it can be helpful for them to build in external accountability to meet internal expectations.

For example, Tim would benefit from a gym buddy to keep him accountable to meeting his personal wellness goal.

3. **Questioner tendency:** Questioners will scrutinize all expectations, both inner and outer expectations. Questioners tend to rely heavily on their rational understanding of a circumstance. If it makes sense, they will accept and meet the expectations. However, if any of the expectations appear arbitrary or unproductive, a questioner will tend to detach from any effort to meet the expectations. Giving a clear and logical *why* goes a long way toward convincing a questioner to meet expectations. For instance, Carole has been told by her administrator that she is not able to do professional development off the school grounds, even if the conference is held remotely. She is frustrated because she knows that she has the integrity to attend all of the remote session offerings, but she doesn't want to waste time commuting to school simply to meet the external expectations of her principal. Carole is also the kind of person who must look at all possible options before choosing how to spend her professional development funds. For a questioner like Carole, it's helpful for her to remember that sometimes, the best thing to do is to make a *good enough* decision.

4. **Rebel tendency:** A rebel tends to push back against any and all expectations, inner and outer. Rebels tend to dislike being told what to do by anyone, regardless of their position within the school's hierarchy. Interestingly, the resistance extends to their own expectations for themselves, which means that they often hinder their own progress and achievement. For instance, Sarah, a rebel, will not sign up with colleagues for a weekend conference too far in the future because she has no idea what she'll feel like doing then. Also, Sarah struggles to meet her fitness goals because when it comes to the moment to get ready to work out, she just doesn't feel like going (even if the goal is important to her, long term). Sarah would do well to alleviate the pressure to meet expectations and simply remind herself, "I want to achieve this goal. This is important to me."

Rubin's (2017) Four Tendencies model provides insights that can help us to anticipate some of the obstacles we might face as we set out to refocus ourselves and set new goals that align with our purpose as educators and individuals. Additionally, once we understand our roadblocks, we can find ways to alleviate the blocks and motivate ourselves to meet our inner and external expectations more readily.

Table 3.1 shows examples of the ways in which educators with each of the Four Tendencies may approach the curricular planning process. Upholders, questioners, obligers, and rebel teachers all approach planning in different ways.

TABLE 3.1: EXAMPLE TENDENCIES FOR CURRICULAR PLANNING

Tendency	Description	Approach to Yearly and Curricular Planning	Helpful Hints to Help Navigate Your Tendency
Upholder	Meets inner and outer expectations without trouble.	Is good at keeping up with planning. *I consistently cross-reference weekly plans with monthly and yearly plans to ensure they align.*	Since this approach works well for planning, keep on track but be sure to embrace the unplanned teachable moments as they come up. Flexibility and spontaneity can lead to powerful learning, too!
Obliger	Meets outward rules but struggles with inward expectations.	Follows curricular obligation with fidelity but sometimes deviates from planning in favor of following someone else's approach. *I always stay true to the mandated curricular outcomes, but I'll scrap my plans if I see something cool on social media or if a colleague across the hall has a better way to approach the lesson.*	This approach is valued by administrators and parents because there is a guarantee that all curricular expectations will be upheld. One area to watch out for is that you may spend countless hours planning a quality unit only to replace it because someone else's lessons seem better. Try not to compare yourself to others; be honest about the quality of your lesson planning and stick to your lessons if they get the job done!

continued →

Tendency	Description	Approach to Yearly and Curricular Planning	Helpful Hints to Help Navigate Your Tendency
Questioner	Questions inner and outer expectations, following through only on what makes sense to them within their particular circumstance.	Sticks to plans as long as they still make sense. *I stay loyal to my yearly plans as long as they connect meaningfully to our interests. I will stray from my plans if they feel arbitrary. I often scrap my weekly plans in favor of following a student's interest or a class inquiry.*	Continue questioning the value of your classroom experiences through the lens of what's best for student learning and for your own sense of balance; however, remember that overthinking a lesson can waste time and precious energy. Sometimes we have to accept that *done* is better than *perfect*.
Rebel	Struggles to meet any expectations or follow rules of any kind, especially if they seem arbitrary.	Rarely follows the curriculum directly and doesn't tend to make a yearly plan. *I rarely focus on long-term curricular planning and tend to be more creative in my approach to planning. I like to play things by ear and go with the flow of the students and classroom. I hate doing the same thing over and over.*	While this approach is freeing, it can also be incredibly stressful. Not knowing what you're teaching day to day or where you're headed in the year can lead to overwhelm. It's a good idea to preplan a few key projects or lesson units throughout each term to pull you through, lessons that incorporate a lot of choice within them. Our students do well with structure and routine, and when the rest of life feels stressful, having some structure at school is good for us as educators, too.

Motivating ourselves, our colleagues, and our students to achieve particular goals can be challenging. While the Four Tendencies framework can give us approaches for maximizing our ability to meet internal and external expectations, it's also helpful to explore the way that rewards and motivators can contribute to the successful achievement of specific goals.

Motivation and Rewards

Setting goals alone won't necessarily ensure that we achieve them. As educators, most of us have spent countless hours figuring out how to motivate our students and ourselves in order to reach targets related to the curriculum, academic objectives, and behavioral goals (Anderman & Anderman, 2014). Many of us learned about motivation through the lens of behavior modification and conditioning approaches during teacher training or have even experienced this approach as we went through the school system, but taking a one-size-fits-all approach to motivation in the classroom and within our own personal lives is ineffective. Instead, it can be helpful to think about differentiating extrinsic and intrinsic reward systems depending on the type of goal or task you want to complete, and connecting our goals to a broader sense of purpose and meaning.

According to Daniel Pink (2009), author of *Drive: The Surprising Truth About What Motivates Us*, tasks can be categorized as either (1) *algorithmic*—routine tasks that are completed over and over again (for instance, taking attendance), or (2) *heuristic*—individual tasks that have no road map, that we have to figure out each time we set out to complete them (for example, planning a unit on a new curricular topic). With regard to motivators, *extrinsic motivators* are external rewards such as money, fame, grades, and praise (Seifert & Sutton, 2009). These types of rewards originate from outside of the individual and are the primary motivator for completing certain tasks. *Intrinsic motivators* arise from within the individual and are often based on meeting our internal needs as opposed to reaping an external reward. According to Pink (2009), extrinsic motivators (money, grades, or praise) work best for algorithmic tasks—the tasks that tend to rely on routine. For instance, encouraging your students to have their pencils and binders ready for learning time every morning might be well served by applying a points system or some other kind of positive extrinsic motivator for those who comply. Intrinsic motivators, however, work best for heuristic tasks that require flexibility, creativity, and deeper-level thinking. For example, inviting students to engage in meaningful writing tends to be better served when we connect the goals to personal growth and a sense of accomplishment, rather than offering a prize for the *best* piece of writing. Often, if one tries to apply extrinsic motivators to heuristic tasks, the result can be decreased motivation for individuals.

Pink (2009) asserts that while external and intrinsic rewards contribute to our ability to meet goals, we are motivated to complete goals related to a third *internal driver* guided by three essential keys: (1) autonomy (the desire to have agency over our own lives), (2) mastery (the ability to increase our ability in tasks over time and through ongoing efforts), and (3) purpose (the desire to set and achieve goals that contribute to something bigger than ourselves).

For example, imagine Jenny has set the heuristic goal of planning a dynamic and engaging unit on number sense in mathematics next term for her students. Achieving the goal of planning intrinsically motivates her because she is proud of her efforts to make learning meaningful and engaging for her students. Additionally, planning connects to her need for autonomy because she gets to choose the approaches and activities for the unit, allows for mastery because she stretches her knowledge and capabilities to develop a strong program for her students, and ties into her broader sense of purpose as she knows this unit will make a difference in the self-efficacy of her students in mathematics long term. In addition to determining whether a task should connect to intrinsic or extrinsic motivators, it is universally motivating when a goal is connected to autonomy, mastery, and a sense of purpose.

Confidence Circles

According to world-renowned author, professor, speaker, and positive psychologist Shawn Achor (2010), building on small successes is the key to achieving our larger goals. Sometimes our ambitions become overwhelming, but Achor suggests breaking larger tasks and goals into small chunks and focusing on only one chunk at a time, building confidence as you move along.

I like to use *confidence circles* as a helpful image for goal setting. Imagine tossing a small pebble in a pool. The ripples start small and grow bigger as they move across the surface of the water. So, when you want to accomplish a large goal, it's helpful to chunk it into smaller, dopamine-friendly parts (Mehta, 2013). If you want to hold mini-conferences with students every day, check off each successful meeting in your daybook or planner. If you want to write report cards at a less stressful pace than usual, commit to writing report cards for just fifteen minutes every day for three weeks, and follow it up with some well-deserved *you* time once you've committed to that goal. If you want to start walking three days a week with colleagues at lunchtime, text one another for accountability in the morning to ensure that it will happen. We can build confidence by starting small and building on those small successes to give us confidence as we move on to other, more daunting tasks.

RAS and Goal Setting

Another important aspect of goal-setting success is derived from our ability to focus our attention on specific, meaningful tasks related to our goals (Chowdhury, 2020). The *reticular activating system* (RAS) is a part of the brain that plays a starring role in determining our goal-related actions (Garcia-Rill, Kezunovic, Hyde, Simon, Beck, & Urbano, 2013). It is a cluster of cells in our brain that filters through the thousands of messages, demands, and attention-sucking stimuli to determine what truly deserves our attention. For example, when we're in the classroom, our RAS filters the nonessential stimuli (for example, the color of pencils your students use or the style of binder they bring to class every day) from the more essential stimulus or information (for instance, the troublesome social dynamics between two students as they walk into your classroom or the note being passed between friends).

Our brain only becomes consciously aware of particular aspects of our surroundings and circumstances if and when it's required to do so. Otherwise, it tends to gloss over the seemingly less important details—essentially sleeping through them. Researchers state that our RAS is directly related to our arousal systems, which have been evolutionarily designed to conserve energy unless there is a specific, safety-related reason to focus our attention (Garcia-Rill et al., 2013).

When we don't have clear SMART goals, our attentiveness toward a desired way of life is low. We fail to access and recognize the steps we need to take, the resources we need to tap, and the opportunities that will bring us closer to where we want to go. Alternatively, when we focus our attention on a few SMART goals, our RAS is activated and conspires to bring our goals to the forefront of our thoughts and attention, making it more likely that we will achieve them (Garcia-Rill et al., 2013).

Procrastination

One of the most challenging roadblocks to success is procrastination. Procrastination is defined as the act of voluntarily delaying an intentional goal despite acknowledging that you'll be worse off for the delay (Klingsieck, 2013). Educators may identify as procrastinators when the time comes for writing lengthy and detailed report card comments, making the tough phone calls to parents after school, or prioritizing back-to-school planning just as the summer beckons us to enjoy the last few beach days. Procrastination allows us to enjoy temporary relief from our stressors, with the understanding that we'll likely pay for it later (Steel, 2011). We procrastinate when we are feeling helpless, anxious, embarrassed, or unhappy, or when we feel like our goal is outside our locus of control (Grunschel, Patrzek, & Fries, 2012).

Many adults are plagued by procrastination and can find it challenging to deviate from their tendency to procrastinate. Those who procrastinate are more likely to have elevated stress levels and lower well-being (Steel, 2011). Approximately 20 percent of adults admit to being chronic procrastinators (Grant, 2016). Procrastination tends to have a negative impact on our ambitions overall (Simpson & Pychyl, 2009).

Procrastination goes beyond the simple inability to manage time effectively. At the core of procrastination lies our difficulty with self-regulating emotions and stressors. Research by DePaul University suggests that there are five main causes of procrastination: conflicting emotions, fear of failure, impulsivity, denial, and rebelliousness (Jaffe, 2013). Procrastination can result in self-sabotage, causing one to fail on a project or goal. Essentially, when we think back on the triggers that cause our brains to go into a fight, flight, or freeze mentality, procrastination is our brain's way of freezing and putting the limbic brakes on a circumstance that is overwhelming us (Shanker, 2017).

One of the easiest ways to overcome procrastination may seem counterintuitive. Researchers have found that giving ourselves a limited, time-specific break from a stressful obligation, goal, or task can invigorate our attention and stamina, reducing our tendency to want to avoid it (Whitbourne, 2018). In his book *When*, Daniel Pink (2018) asserts the need for regular breaks, what he calls *vigilance breaks*, from cognitively exhausting work in order to recharge and reinvigorate ourselves to do our best work. Chunking tasks into small parts also helps with overwhelm, in turn reducing the likelihood that we'll put off our ambitious goals (Shatté, 2015). When we see our goals as doable, our confidence increases, and our likelihood of completing them rises (Amabile & Kramer, 2011). Often our overwhelm can be fueled by negative self-talk, which can lead to procrastination. Tap into some of the positive affirmations from chapter 2 (page 37) to reframe your self-talk. Try to keep that inner dialogue positive as you approach daunting tasks!

The next section outlines six specific ways to increase your ability to meet your objectives.

The Secrets of Goal Success

Following the SMART goals framework (see page 76) and aligning your goals in such a way that they optimize your overall internal motivation tendencies (see page 83) are important factors in achieving your targets, professionally or personally, within your own life. Additionally, there are several things you can do to maximize your successes when it comes to goal success.

- Write down your goals.
- Identify your values.
- Prioritize goal-related tasks.
- Create categories.
- Anchor your accountability.
- Think about timing.

Write Down Your Goals

One of the easiest ways you can be successful in hitting your targets is to alert your RAS—that tiny part of your brain that screams at you to pay attention!—by writing your goals down. According to a study by Gail Matthews (2015), individuals who write down their goals are 33 percent more likely to achieve them compared to their counterparts who simply rely on keeping their goals in their heads. The act of identifying goals clearly and writing them down activates your brain to focus on the goal you have written down. Educators don't need to spend a lot of time or effort formulating goals; just the simple act of writing targets down can make it more likely that you'll be successful.

Identify Your Values

According to research, values are influential factors and contributors to our overall achievement and growth (Farber, 2012). While values are not goals, they represent the inner compass that informs *where* we want to *go* in our lives, our hypothetical *direction* as educators. Our values signify what we believe in, reflect our moral views, indicate what matters to us, guide how we interact with others, and form the legacy we wish to leave behind (Farber, 2012).

Most educators have strong core values that illuminate their personal and professional lives. Values are less about setting specific targets and more about determining how we want to act moving forward (Farber, 2012). According to Brené Brown, you really only have one to two core values that guide everything in your life, even if you identify with ten or twenty of the values that exist. The importance of identifying your primary core values is that you can align your secondary values underneath them. Use the following five steps to identify your primary core values.

1. Read through the list of values presented in figure 3.2.

2. Circle all the values that resonate with you on the list (you'll likely circle ten to twenty). List them in a journal, on scrap paper, or in your phone.

3. Categorize the values according to any themes or patterns you observe. Often, many of our secondary values are guided by a central theme or primary core value.

4. From the patterns, identify one or two values that jump out at you or seem to have recurred throughout the exercise. These are your primary or core values. Make note of these words.

5. Reflect on your values as you set and reflect upon your goals. Ask yourself the following.

   • "What are the values that inform my goals and drive my purpose as an educator and in my personal life?"

   • "Am I living up to my values day to day in my role as an educator and in my personal life?"

   • "How can I use my values to keep pushing for growth as an educator and in my personal life?"

Prioritize Your Goal-Related Tasks

When you are overwhelmed, you can feel off-balance. Quite often, educators desperately seek work-life balance, but evidence has shown that the illusion of balance can be more damaging than helpful (Schwingshackl, 2014). Perfect balance in a busy life is not an attainable goal. Instead, it might be more helpful to adopt a mindset that strives for work-life *fit* or *flexibility*—the notion that the demands on your resources (time, attention, and money) ebb and flow and that you can adjust your own approach and pace to task completion accordingly (Vengapally, 2019). Prioritizing tasks according to importance is one alternative to the futile attempt to acquire work-life balance because it gives you peace of mind knowing which tasks are urgent, which are important, and which can be pushed aside for a later time.

Achievement	Compassion	Gratitude	Meaningful Work	Self-Respect
Adventure	Competency	Growth	Openness	Service
Altruism	Connection	Happiness	Optimism	Spirituality
Ambition	Contribution	Honesty	Peace	Stability
Authenticity	Cooperation	Humor	Pleasure	Status
Authority	Creativity	Influence	Poise	Success
Autonomy	Curiosity	Inner Harmony	Popularity	Time
Balance	Determination	Justice	Recognition	Trustworthiness
Beauty	Fairness	Kindness	Religion	Understanding
Belonging	Faith	Knowledge	Reputation	Uniqueness
Boldness	Fame	Leadership	Respect	Wealth
Challenge	Freedom	Learning	Responsibility	Well-being
Citizenship	Friendships	Love	Security	Wisdom
Community	Fun	Loyalty		

Source: Adapted from Brown, 2018; Clear, 2020.

Figure 3.2: List of values.

*Visit **go.SolutionTree.com/teacherefficacy** for a free reproducible version of this figure.*

In a 1954 speech, former U.S. president Dwight D. Eisenhower said that there are two types of problems in the world: the urgent and the important. The urgent problems, he went on to state, tend not to be important, and the important problems never seem urgent. Important tasks require forward thinking and often contribute to us meeting our goals, professionally or personally. Urgent responsibilities require us to take immediate action and often relate to meeting the demands placed on us by others. Urgent tasks often take up most of our attention because not addressing them often results in troubling and immediate consequences.

Eisenhower urged people to become efficient and effective time managers by prioritizing the important tasks before they become urgent so we never find ourselves in a circumstance when we are faced with an overwhelming number of tight deadlines. To manage your resources effectively and stop putting yourself in a position where you are always fighting fires, you first need to identify which activities are urgent and which are important.

Stephen Covey, author of the acclaimed book *The Seven Habits of Highly Effective People*, extrapolated Eisenhower's thoughts and created a helpful matrix to delineate the ways in which you can prioritize your tasks (see table 3.2).

TABLE 3.2: URGENT AND IMPORTANT TASKS MATRIX

	Urgent	Non-urgent
Important	Crises **MUST DO NOW**	Goals and Planning **IDEAL**
Not Important	Interruptions **DECREASE**	Distractions **ELIMINATE**

Source: Adapted from Covey, 1989.

- *Urgent and important tasks* need your immediate attention because they are usually crises and result in massive negative consequences if they are not addressed quickly. This firefighting mode can lead you directly to burnout if you're not careful. If you are running from one important and urgent task to another all day long, you don't give yourself enough breathing room to make plans and anticipate the future.

- *Important and non-urgent tasks* tend to be related to goal setting and planning. This is an ideal place within which to make decisions because you have time to make the right ones based on integrity and values. Addressing these tasks requires discipline and forward thinking.

- *Not important, urgent tasks* often require you to solve them immediately but are the types of problems you could address or reduce with better planning. Outsourcing these tasks or planning ahead to decrease these tasks is important.

- *Not important, non-urgent tasks* tend to cause low stress, and you can often remove them completely from your workflow once you've identified them appropriately.

It can be challenging to determine which priorities are important and urgent compared to the ones lower down on the hierarchy. Many educators are dedicated to their role in the classroom and often treat all tasks as urgent and important.

This can be unhealthy and lead to burnout. One easy way to conceptualize professional and personal responsibilities is to imagine that you are juggling balls, some made of glass and others made of rubber. It's easier to juggle many balls when you know which ones you can drop. Rubber balls bounce. Glass balls shatter. The rubber balls represent tasks that you can easily put aside without significant consequence to your well-being and livelihood, while the glass balls are so essential to your life that you cannot drop them without major repercussions. The balls you juggle could be your friends, family, romantic relationships, work and career, personal growth, spirituality, health and wellness, and leisure time activities. At different points in your life, the balls take on a different relative importance to one another—some are glass at certain times, and at other times, some are rubber.

When I think of my own glass balls, I consider family, health, and my educator role my glass balls, while some of the other parts of my life are rubber balls and can be dropped once in a while.

Glass or Rubber?

How can we determine which balls are glass and which balls are rubber? Here are some questions to consider as you identify the various responsibilities in your life.

- What is the long-term impact of dropping this ball?
- Who is impacted by this ball?
- If I dropped this ball, would I recuperate?
- Is this ball even mine to juggle?
- What are the benefits of this ball in my life?

Create Categories

Creating categories of values-based goals related to your work life or personal life can reduce a sense of overwhelm, provide clarity, and offer direction. For example, it might be helpful to group your goals (and subsequent values) around particular themes, such as family and friendships, spiritual or religious beliefs, work and career, health and well-being, education and learning, and fun and leisure (see figure 3.3, page 92). Under each theme, you might want to indicate one or two goals to focus on in the short term and the long term. Beginning your goals with a verb makes them more action oriented.

Family, Friendships, and Relationships	Spiritual Beliefs
Short-Term: Spend next Saturday morning going to the park and playing with my own children.	Short-Term: Spend three minutes focusing on my breath every morning before the bell rings.
Long-Term: Commit to a monthly after-school get-together with my colleagues.	Long-Term: Make time every week to take a gratitude walk.
Work and Career	**Health and Well-Being**
Short-Term: Find new and engaging physical education games for my class related to cooperation.	Short-Term: Walk three times this week during lunch or recess.
Long-Term: Plan for a grade change for next year; start reading up on the curriculum for grade 10.	Long-Term: Sign up and train for the 10K community run in the spring with some colleagues.
Education and Learning	**Fun and Leisure**
Short-Term: Sign up for the next district professional development seminar on literacy.	Short-Term: Finish editing my fall family photos for the annual photobook this month.
Long-Term: Begin my master's in educational leadership next September.	Long-Term: Plan my winter family trip to Mexico this month.

Figure 3.3: Example of category-based goals.

Use the reproducible "My Category-Based Goals" (page 103) as a template to record your own category-based goals.

Anchor Your Accountability

Regardless of your motivational tendency (upholder, rebel, or otherwise; see page 78), researchers have found that anchoring your goals to external systems of accountability increases your overall ability to meet your targets, professionally and personally. According to Gail Matthews (2015), more than 70 percent of research participants who sent weekly goal updates to an accountability buddy reported achieving their goals compared to those who kept their goals to themselves. Tapping into the benefits of an accountability partner can be tremendously helpful in keeping you focused on your targets (Matthews, 2015).

An accountability partner is a person who is dedicated to helping you reach your goals, someone you become answerable to when it comes to meeting some of the micro-goals you have set for yourself (Harvard Business Review, 2019). Often, these arrangements work well if there is a level of give and take, such that you become as invested in your partner's goals as your partner is in yours. For instance, when you're working hard to complete assessments and report card comments, if you only answer to yourself, it can be easy to procrastinate or allow your commitment to slide in favor of that new Netflix special or the social media rabbit hole. Instead, an accountability partner gently reminds you of and encourages you to stay committed to your goals. When it comes to accountability partners, it's important that they are dependable, share your work ethic, and understand the importance of your goals as they relate to your values and future vision for your life.

Think About Timing

When you set goals for yourself, it's important to consider timing and scheduling as contributing factors to your success by examining your *timing personality* and by *batching* your efforts.

Timing Personalities

According to author Dan Pink (2018), individuals have three main chronographs or *timing personalities* that can determine the ideal time of day for productive, routine, or creative tasks. These include the lark (early bird), the owl (late riser), and the combination of both types. Sometimes, our time tendencies are influenced by age (just think how early toddlers tend to wake up or how late teenagers generally rise in the morning), but generally, three-quarters of us, Pink asserts, tend to be larks (early risers). Knowing your own timing personality is helpful, as it can enable you to schedule particular tasks during certain times of the day in your classrooms and in your own life.

Pink (2018) explains that each of us experiences a peak, trough, and recovery phase each day, which depends on our chronograph (timing personality). The peak is our most productive, high-energy period of the day, when we are best able to problem solve and complete our most difficult mental work. For instance, this is the point in the day when I like to teach complex concepts like writing and mathematics to my students with a sense of urgency and charisma, responding quickly to their needs. The trough is characterized by low energy and challenges completing difficult mental tasks. During this time, my lower-energy state benefits from quieter, more relaxed, and gentler routines, such as silent reading, art, and even some of the more routine tasks like writing in our agendas or doing printing practice. The recovery tends to be an effective time for creativity because we experience a loosening of the logical, rational approach to thinking and a more fluid, creative mindset as we recover from the low-energy trough. I find it easier to plan units and lessons during this time, since I'm in a more creative mindset.

Depending on your timing personality, the peak, trough, and recovery periods differ. For the lark, the peak period tends to be first thing in the morning, so planning more rigorous work, meetings, and teaching more challenging concepts first thing in the morning makes sense. The trough period usually comes after lunch around one o'clock for the lark, so it makes sense to plan more routine tasks for this period, such as filling in forms, cleaning, or sorting paperwork. The recovery phase is generally something larks experience into the afternoon and evening, so carving out some time to get creative at that time might offer some benefits to your overall well-being as educators. For the owl, however, the trough period is usually first thing in the morning, which means owls should really reserve routine tasks for that period of time. The peak and recovery come later in the day and late into the evening.

It can be helpful to plan your days knowing that not all tasks and time blocks are created equal.

Time Blocks and Batching

Often, you can maximize your overall productivity by planning to complete your goals within significant and generous time blocks. Additionally, there are benefits to batching similar tasks because it allows you to focus more effectively on your goals in a deeper way (Kresser, 2017). As author and world-renowned photographer Chase Jarvis states in his book *Creative Calling* (2019), "It requires discipline to maintain boundaries and not let the other kind of work spill in, but batching is a masterful way to protect creative work from the day-to-day interruptions that feel urgent but actually aren't and can easily wait until you are ready to deal with them" (p. 137).

Multitasking destroys productivity. In fact, researcher and neuroscientist Clifford Nass stated in an NPR interview that multitasking should be called *multi-switching* because it is impossible for us to truly focus on more than one task simultaneously; therefore, when we attempt to focus on multiple things at once, we are really just switching between tasks quickly (Flatow, 2013). The problem with trying to consistently chip away at a goal in twenty- to thirty-minute increments is that it can take up to several minutes to establish your mindset and focus yourself in these smaller time blocks. Naturally, the rapid-fire switching leads to a remarkable loss of productivity.

As a result, research suggests that dedicated time blocks of ninety minutes are ideal for tackling big goals. For example, if you are planning to spend a weekend writing report cards, it's best to work hard on them for ninety minutes straight, giving yourself small social media, email, or social breaks as opposed to keeping your email tab open and phone within reach and trying to bounce between distractions while you write.

As a busy, full-time educator and mother, I don't have a lot of expendable time during evenings and weekends once the children are fed, bathed, and put to bed; the lunches are made; the lessons are planned; and the schoolwork is marked. Instead of trying to chip away at the production of my podcast, *KindSight 101*, on a weekly basis, I often choose several days a month or during holiday break to record interviews with guests. The batching approach allows me to juggle the important balls instead of scrambling to keep too many balls in the air unsuccessfully.

Strategies to Ignite Your Refocusing Fire

This section of the chapter includes three main parts that will support a successful approach to refocusing your ambitions and setting realistic, achievable goals: (1) strategies for laying the groundwork, (2) strategies for exploring timing and scheduling, and (3) strategies for maintaining your motivation, to keep the fire going. Goal setting is an important aspect of meeting your emotional need for personal growth, and being successful in your ambitions requires an intentional, thoughtful approach.

Laying the Groundwork Strategies

This section will lay a strong foundation for your goals through the Painting Your Future: Vision Board exercise and by exploring a specific goal-setting template.

Painting Your Future: Vision Board Exercise

If you want to make significant changes to the status quo in your life, professionally as a teacher or personally, it can be helpful to incorporate visualization into your approach to goal setting. One of my favorite ways to create a concrete picture of the future is to create a vision board. A vision board is tool for visualization created from a collage of meaningful letters, words, images, and symbols that represent your goals and hopes for the future. One of the most effective ways to use a vision board is to keep it visible and revisit it often. Doing so will activate your RAS, signaling that you should pay special attention to the goal. Use the following three steps to make your vision board.

1. **Set the intention:** Start by thinking about a goal you want for yourself. Visualize your goal in painstaking detail by reflecting on some of the following questions as though you have achieved your goal.

- When did you achieve the goal?

- How did it feel to achieve the goal?

- What are you doing now that you have achieved your goal?

- What does your schedule look like now that you have achieved your goal?

- Who are you meant to be?

- What do you wish your legacy to be?

- How do you want your relationships to be?

2. **Visualize:** Look for images, photos, and magazines that represent the sentiments, vision, possessions, experiences, and people you wish to have in your life as a result of your goal. You can use words, affirmations, quotes, and small symbols (keys, buttons, and stickers) to add depth and texture to the vision board.

3. **Revisit:** Find a prominent place in your home where you will display the board until the goal is achieved. Celebrate your successes and keep coming back to the goal daily by looking at your vision board.

Goal-Setting Template Exercise

Review the nine-step directions that follow before filling out the "Goal-Setting Template" on page 104. Figure 3.4 contains an example goal-setting template.

1. **Take stock of your values:** For this exercise, use a journal or even your phone to take stock of the two primary values you identified in figure 3.2 (page 89) that guide your actions and secondary values, professionally and personally.

2. **Categorize your goals:** Now, think about the main categories in your life and choose three main areas you'd like to focus on for the purpose of this exercise. Where do you see yourself (in the context of these categories) in the future?

3. **Narrow down your goals:** Next, make a list of all the big goals you have for yourself in the three main categories of your life. For example, you may want to focus on three of the following themes: family, friendships, and relationships; spiritual beliefs; work and career; health and well-being; education and learning; and fun and leisure. Choose three big goals that stick out for you, goals that seem most important

Goal 1	Goal 2	Goal 3
Spend four nights a week sitting down for dinner with my family.	Complete two courses toward my master's in educational leadership within the first term of the next school year.	Jog around my neighborhood twice a week for thirty minutes in the morning.
Life Category: Family	Life Category: Education and Learning	Life Category: Health and Well-being
How does this goal connect with my values? Why is it significant to me? Spending time with my family is related to the way that I value connection. It is essential that I maintain connection with my family.	How does this goal connect with my values? Why is it significant to me? I value growth in my personal life and professional life. In order to achieve a sense of growth, I like to set ambitious and exciting goals for my learning.	How does this goal connect with my values? Why is it significant to me? A healthy lifestyle is important to me because it helps me achieve a sense of inner harmony. Morning jogging is a good way to clear my head and move my body.
Short-Term Goal: Sit down for dinner four nights a week for the next two weeks. Long-Term Goal: Aim for a consistent schedule of at least sitting down to dinner three nights a week, depending on activities, within six months' time.	Short-Term Goal: Register for the master's in educational leadership program by January, ensuring that all items on the application proposal are complete. Long-Term Goal: Complete the master's in educational leadership two years from my start date.	Short-Term Goal: Set my alarm thirty minutes earlier than usual and walk around my neighborhood on Tuesdays and Thursdays for two weeks starting tomorrow. Long-Term Goal: Start jogging on Tuesday and Thursday mornings for thirty minutes during the next three months.
Success will look like . . . My family will be spending quality time together at meals for twenty to thirty minutes more frequently than before. Success will feel like . . . I will feel proud of and connected to my family.	Success will look like . . . I will be learning and reading about school-related topics that grow my knowledge and career. Success will feel like . . . I will feel accomplished and proud to have followed through on my goal.	Success will look like . . . I will be waking up early and committing to my goal of running or walking two mornings per week. Success will feel like . . . I will feel happy and calm after my walks, which will help give me a sense of inner harmony.

Figure 3.4: Example detailed goal-setting template.

continued →

I can anticipate my roadblocks will be . . .	I can anticipate my roadblocks will be . . .	I can anticipate my roadblocks will be . . .
• The children will be busy with activities. • My spouse will be busy with work. • I will be overwhelmed with planning and marking. I can counteract these roadblocks proactively by . . . • Decreasing prep time by ordering in one of the days. • Scheduling activities before or after dinner time. • Ensuring that both my spouse and I will have time to catch up on work after the mealtime.	• It will be hard to feel motivated to do schoolwork during the week. • It will be challenging to squeeze in studying during my already busy schedule. • I might feel guilty about the extra financial and time costs associated with school. I can counteract these roadblocks proactively by . . . • Reminding myself with a mantra that my goal is important long-term will help motivate me. • Asking my spouse, a babysitter, or a family member to help me with childcare will free up extra time to complete assignments. • Reminding myself that eventually the financial cost and scheduling challenges will be worth it because I will be earning more.	• It will be challenging to wake up early on the rainy and cold days. • It will be difficult to start running when I don't feel motivated to run. • My children often rely on me in the morning, which will make it tricky to sneak away. I can counteract these roadblocks proactively by . . . • Setting my clothes out the night before, so I am ready for the morning. • Purchasing appropriate rain gear so I am warm and comfortable, even when the weather is not ideal. • Allowing myself to run intermittently on challenging days to enable me to feel more motivated. • Asking my spouse to cover the two mornings per week.
Who will help me? • My children • My spouse • The restaurant	Who will help me? • My extended family • My spouse • My babysitter	Who will help me? • My children • My spouse
What do I need? • A clear schedule • A family meeting to discuss an agreement	What do I need? • A financial budget and payment solution plan • A clear schedule • Support from individuals who can provide childcare	What do I need? • An alarm • Appropriate exercise gear

to you right in this moment. Ensure that you frame them using SMART-goal language.

4. **Find your why:** How might it feel to achieve these goals? How might these goals help align you better with your values? Identify how these goals contribute to a sense of purpose and meaning.

5. **Chunk your goals:** Then, think of some ways you might be able to chunk your overarching goal into a short-term action goal and a long-term one? Identify a smaller, dopamine-friendly short-term and long-term goal for each of the three bigger goals.

6. **Define success:** Take a moment to visualize each of the goals being achieved. What does success look like? What does success feel like to you? How will you know that you have achieved your goal?

7. **Identify the roadblocks and solutions:** Give yourself a chance to examine your motivation tendency (see page 78) and circumstances outside of your control that might contribute to roadblocks on the road to achieving your goal. What are some of the ways you could anticipate the issues and solve them quickly?

8. **Find your accountability network:** Find someone with whom you can share your goal-setting journey, someone who will help you to stay motivated, and someone who cares about your success as much as you do.

9. **Meet your need:** Identify your resource needs and where you'll source the necessary tools and find the resources you need.

Continue revisiting your goals over the coming days, weeks, months, and years.

Timing and Scheduling Strategy

This section introduces the five-second habit hack, which will enable you to move toward your goals, even when your heart's not in it.

Five-Second Habit Hack

Have you ever set a goal or resolution for yourself, only to hesitate when it came to the moment of action? Procrastination and self-sabotage can be tough barriers to overcome when achieving our goals and creating habits of well-being. Research has found that there is a crucial momentary window between the instant we have the desire to do something and the action required to make the aspiration a reality (Krockow, 2018; Soon, Brass, Heinze, & Haynes, 2008). The truth is, when you set your mind to something, the longer you hesitate to do it, the less likely you are to realize it.

According to author and speaker Mel Robbins (2017), acting in the first five seconds after a decision is the key to maintaining motivation, following through on our goals, and increasing the likelihood that we'll complete the task. She's coined this approach the *Five-Second Rule*. What the Five-Second Rule allows you to do is act on the desire immediately, capitalize on your motivation and self-efficacy, and move toward the goal before your rational brain tries to talk you out of it! As author, entrepreneur, and speaker Seth Godin (2007) asserts, now is better than soon. Sometimes, you need to stop *thinking* and simply take *action* toward your goals.

Here's how it works in three steps.

1. Make a decision related to a goal or a habit you would like to adopt in your life. For example, you decide that you're going to go for a lunchtime walk every weekday at lunch with teacher colleagues.

2. When the moment of action arrives and you feel yourself hesitate to act, count down: "Five, four, three, two, one, GO." Imagine that the lunch bell has rung on the first Monday after you've made your decision to start your new lunchtime walking routine. Suddenly, you feel pulled by the stack of marking towering on your desk. You feel hesitation wash over you. In this moment, you count, "Five, four, three, two, one, GO" (Robbins, 2017).

3. Take physical action toward your goal. Stand up and grab your sneakers. The simple act of grabbing your shoes, backed by your intention, will be enough to counteract the inner voice convincing you to stay to finish your marking instead.

Keeping the Fire Burning Strategies

Now that you have created a clear vision, a distinct set of goals, and a strategy to overcome procrastination, it's important to examine the success of your goals and enact a strategy to stay motivated. In this section, you will learn how to determine whether a goal is worthwhile pursuing through the 2×2 strategy, and you will explore a simple and effective ten-minute accountability exercise you can implement immediately to get closer to achieving your goals.

Quit or Commit? The 2×2 Strategy

There are times when quitting a goal is the best thing you can do for yourself. Letting go of goals can allow you to refocus on juggling only the most important glass balls. As Seth Godin asserts in his 2007 book *The Dip*, for every goal we have there is always a hard part. We must determine whether we are going to quit or whether we are going to keep going depending on the *type* of hard we encounter.

One type of challenge is *the cul-de-sac*, which literally means the dead end (Godin, 2007). It's the goal for which, no matter how much you throw at it, nothing seems to improve. Imagine that your goal is to collaborate more frequently with your grade-group partner, but after countless attempts to reach out, you are met with resistance and coldness. It may be time to release yourself from the goal to work with him. Perhaps you may be better served to choose a colleague at a different grade level with whom to work.

Another type of difficulty you can encounter when trying to meet a goal is *the dip*. The dip, Godin (2007) asserts, is what happens after the excitement of setting a goal has worn off; it's the challenge of actually putting in the hard work even when you don't feel like it. Success feels uncertain, but often, if you simply push through, you can achieve success through incremental, hard work.

Chris Guillebeau, a world-renowned coach, author, and speaker on non-conformity who teaches others how to tap into their creativity and life purpose, swears by the 2×2 strategy to determine whether he should continue with a goal, tweak a goal, or re-evaluate his pursuit of a goal (Jarvis, 2020). He encourages his students to reflect on the following two questions.

1. Is it working?

2. Do I love it?

Use the 2×2 matrix in figure 3.5 to determine the best path forward.

	It is working.	It is not working.
I love it.	It's working, and I love it. **Keep going!**	It's not working, but I love it. **How can you tweak the goal to be more effective?**
I do not love it.	It's working, but I don't love it. **What can you tweak to make the goal more enjoyable?**	It's not working, and I don't love it. **Quit or refocus the goal!**

Figure 3.5: "Is it working or not?" matrix.

Refocus Rescue: Ten-Minute Accountability Exercise

At the beginning of my return to school in the fall of 2020, after nearly seven months out of the classroom due to COVID-19, my teacher friend, Jodie Labelle, and I decided to support one another with our respective goals for the year, knowing how challenging and stressful the year was gearing up to be due to added health and safety protocols, ever-changing community stressors related to COVID-19, and concerns of worried parents. We decided to start our week with a positive phone call every Monday morning at 6 a.m. We agreed to a strict ten-minute timeline for the weekly morning phone calls so we could realistically keep our commitment to one another. It has been one of the most effective ways to keep my goals clear and my motivation high. Additionally, talking to my friend always makes for a positive start to the week. We continue to make these phone calls a priority every Monday morning without exception. Here is the four-step accountability exercise.

1. Choose a colleague or friend who seems committed to setting and achieving goals for the future. It helps if this person is dependable and goal oriented.

2. Schedule your weekly call, keeping in mind the need for clear timeline boundaries and creative solutions for working around your non-negotiable responsibilities.

3. Decide who will make the call each week and commit to the goal.

4. During the phone call, ensure that both partners have a chance to voice their goals for the week and reflect on the past week's successes or challenges.

Conclusion

Throughout the course of this chapter, you have examined the important aspects of goal setting, including your psychology, the roadblocks, the ways in which you can maximize your productivity and efficacy, and your psychological motivations when it comes to reaching your highest ambitions. After all, part of the reason educators feel burnt out is that we lack purpose and a deep sense of connection to the work we do in the classroom as well as to our bigger-picture goals for ourselves as human beings. This chapter has offered a variety of tactical approaches to goal setting, productivity enhancers, and ways to refocus your professional and personal goals in order to become the teacher you always hoped you could be.

My Category-Based Goals

Family, Friendships, and Relationships	Spiritual Beliefs
Short-Term:	Short-Term:
Long-Term:	Long-Term:
Work and Career	**Health and Well-Being**
Short-Term:	Short-Term:
Long-Term:	Long-Term:
Education and Learning	**Fun and Leisure**
Short-Term:	Short-Term:
Long-Term:	Long-Term:

Goal-Setting Template

Review the nine-step directions on page 96 before filling out the following table.

Goal 1	Goal 2	Goal 3
Life Category:	Life Category:	Life Category:
How does this goal connect with my values? Why is it significant to me?	How does this goal connect with my values? Why is it significant to me?	How does this goal connect with my values? Why is it significant to me?
Short-Term Goal: Long-Term Goal:	Short-Term Goal: Long-Term Goal:	Short-Term Goal: Long-Term Goal:

Success will look like . . .	Success will look like . . .	Success will look like . . .
Success will feel like . . .	Success will feel like . . .	Success will feel like . . .
I can anticipate my roadblocks will be . . .	I can anticipate my roadblocks will be . . .	I can anticipate my roadblocks will be . . .
I can counteract these roadblocks proactively by . . .	I can counteract these roadblocks proactively by . . .	I can counteract these roadblocks proactively by . . .
Who will help me?	Who will help me?	Who will help me?
What do I need?	What do I need?	What do I need?

Page 2 of 2

RECONNECT 4

How to Boost the Quality of the Social Connections in Your Life

The only way we will survive is by being kind. The only way we can get by in this world is through the help we receive from others. No one can do it alone, no matter how great the machines are.

—Amy Poehler

As educators (and adults, specifically), we often take our perspective and *knowing* about others for granted. At times, we forget to see the world through fresh perspectives, allowing ourselves to examine and question what we *think* we know. It turns out that challenging our assumptions and beliefs is one of the most important things we can do to create connections with others, enabling us to lead happy, fulfilled lives as educators.

In this chapter, you will explore the research, strategies, and reflective questions that enable you to foster social awareness and relationship skills as educators to contribute to the well-being of the people in your school. You will learn three tactical ways to build rapport with those around you; how to build positive cultures; three ways to foster a sense of trust with your colleagues, friends, and family members; and how to contribute positive recognition in an effective way using the two-by-ten strategy. To be a fired-up educator, you need to be able to prioritize and nurture interactions with the people in your life.

What the Research Says About Reconnecting

As Shawn Achor states in his 2010 book, *The Happiness Advantage*, much of our success and happiness as individuals is rooted in our human relationships. In fact, social connections are some of the best predictors of success, health, and even life expectancy (Achor, 2010). When it comes to our social-emotional competence, social awareness and relationship skills are two important foundations that enable us to navigate our experiences with others effectively (CASEL, 2020).

Social awareness is the capacity to understand various viewpoints and lived experiences, show empathy and compassion for others, see people from a strengths-based perspective, and show concern for people's emotions (CASEL, 2020). Honing our relationship skills is also an important part of developing social competence. It involves communicating effectively, creating rapport, building on positive relationships, working through conflicts effectively, demonstrating leadership, seeking help and asking for support, and standing up for what we believe in when it comes to social justice and equity (CASEL, 2020).

The Differences Among Empathy, Compassion, and Kindness

Acquiring meaningful lasting friendships, productive and reciprocal collegial relationships, and broad social networks begins with your own willingness to truly see, hear, and understand those in your midst (Umphrey & Sherblom, 2018). You must begin with empathy, compassion, and an eagerness to bravely step into kindness. You need to cultivate the capacity to make generous assumptions and question the default narratives you attribute to those with whom you live, learn, and work (Matthews, 2019). You need to tune into your professional and personal relationships to get the most out of your teaching and personal lives.

Empathy, compassion, and kindness are conduits for connection (Matthews, 2019). If we can take others' perspectives, sit alongside and support individuals as they struggle, and offer acts of kindness to those around us, we have the capacity to build strong bonds with colleagues, students, and parents, which is essential for good communication and overall efficacy, both professionally and personally (McQuaid, 2018). It's easy to get confused when it comes to differentiating among empathy, compassion, and kindness, especially when they are used interchangeably in mainstream society (for examples, see table 4.1, page 110).

In the interest of clarity, I will briefly differentiate empathy, compassion, and kindness, as my friend, author, and school counsellor Barbara Gruener explained them to me (as cited in Michael, 2018a).

- *Empathy* is the practice of understanding someone's feelings and circumstances with your head—putting yourself in the other person's shoes. In doing so, you rethink the assumptions you might already have about people and think critically about the ways you interact with the people in your life, whether they are different from you in terms of age, ethnicity, gender, sexual orientation, physical appearance, culture, economic background, health, or personal experiences.

- *Compassion* is about understanding someone's feelings with your heart. Compassion literally means *to suffer with* (Online Etymology Dictionary, n.d.). In other words, compassion takes the brain-based understanding we have developed through empathy and moves it to our hearts. When we hear people's personal stories, we often connect to their struggles or triumphs with our hearts. According to Gruener, when we can see ourselves in one another, it becomes easier to be compassionate to those who are different from us (Michael, 2018a). When we see the world this way, we ultimately feel more compelled to act to help those in need.

- *Kindness* is being willing to act (with your hands) on your deep empathy and compassion and show up for someone. Often, after hearing or viewing the news online, it can be easy to become overwhelmed by the sadness and negativity you see. You might find yourself feeling a deep sense of empathy and compassion for people suffering through difficult times of war, disaster, or injustice, but then feel paralyzed by a feeling of helplessness and hopelessness. It's easy to watch the news and read your Twitter feed, asking yourself helplessly, "What can *I* do?" or "What can *any of us* do?" Sometimes, this sentiment is referred to as *compassion fatigue* or empathic distress (Coles, 2021; Dowling, 2018). The burden of carrying someone else's pain can feel overwhelming and incredibly heavy. Apathy can replace the hopelessness, driven by a deeply held belief that there's nothing you can do to improve a situation. It's as though you turn emotions *off* or numb them out.

The truth is, as empathy expert Michele Borba states, latent empathy and compassion do no good (Gruener, 2019). It's only when you are able to harness their power by taking meaningful kind action that you can transform the world and affect positive change through small acts (Borba, 2017).

You find kindness in the micro-moments; it is rooted in action (Michael, 2018a). Kindness is the greatest expression of humanity, and it is accessible to all, regardless of age, creed, or race (Keltner, 2012). Kindness is contagious, and it can change the world (Zaki, 2016). Table 4.1 illustrates the differences among empathy, compassion, and kindness.

TABLE 4.1: ILLUSTRATING EMPATHY, COMPASSION, AND KINDNESS

	Empathy	**Compassion**	**Kindness**
Definition	Understanding someone's feelings and circumstances	Connecting emotionally to someone's feelings and circumstances	Using empathy and compassion to take action to effect positive change
Example	A student forgets his homework three days in a row. You demonstrate empathy by taking his perspective, remembering how challenging life must feel since his mom has been sick in the hospital this week.	Through tears, a student in your middle school class informs you that she and her father do not currently have a permanent residence, and she camps in a nearby park every night. Learning that she is homeless makes your heart ache as you listen to her story.	A family at your school has experienced a devastating house fire just weeks before the winter holiday season. Although no one was hurt, all the family's valuables were destroyed. Your school comes together to plan a successful fundraiser that helps get family members back on their feet.

Is Kindness Contagious?

You might have heard that you can influence people's happiness, physiologically, just by being kind (Brodrick, 2019). Kindness ripples outward from the original act and touches people in ways you might not even imagine. Research finds that kindness is contagious, and it comes down to hormones and physiology (Piper, Saslow, & Saturn, 2015). As a result, mobilizing kindness in schools and organizations can be one of the most accessible, significant, and effective tools for positively influencing culture and decreasing the negative effects of burnout (Zaki, 2016).

The Science of Kindness: The Helper's High

There are four important hormones identified as causing happiness or a *helper's high* because of kindness (Breuning, 2016).

1. **Endorphins:** Doing a good deed has the same effect on your body as exercise does. Endorphins, which are your body's natural painkiller, are often called the runner's high. They rush into your bloodstream, making you feel joyful.

2. **Oxytocin:** Oxytocin increases your feeling of social connection, belonging, and optimism. It's responsible for the feelings of love and empathy, being able to put yourself in someone's shoes. It's that same feeling you get when you give someone a hug. Oxytocin is also the chemical responsible for the immediate love between parents and their newborn babies.

3. **Serotonin:** Serotonin boosts your mood, making you feel happy and calm.

4. **Dopamine:** Dopamine gives you the feeling of achievement or reward after achieving a goal.

Our bodies and brains are wired for generosity, and we can literally become happier by doing good deeds (Brodrick, 2019). Here's where kindness has the power to shift culture. When you engage in kindness, your brain releases oxytocin and the other *happiness hormones*, boosting your mood and offering a host of other health-related benefits, including increased heart health, optimism, and a sense of efficacy (Rowland, 2018). Due to the mirror neurons in our brains, the receiver of the kindness also gets an increase in oxytocin (Breuning, 2016). But here's the kicker: the positive hormone surge is not limited to the giver and the receiver. Even someone who *witnesses* generosity gets a dose of happiness hormones (Rowland, 2018). Think back to those heartwarming videos on YouTube that show people doing nice things for one another. That heartwarming feeling is oxytocin coursing through your veins (Breuning, 2016).

Mirror Neurons: Monkey See, Monkey Do

Mirror neurons are the neural mechanisms that enable humans to imitate each other to learn from and connect with one another (Heyes, 2009). In the 1990s, a group of scientists from the University of Parma in Italy discovered that primates learn from one another through imitation, largely thanks to the presence of mirror neurons in their brains (Heyes, 2009). This concept reinforces the commonly used phrase, *Monkey see, monkey do.* This also describes the way babies study the people around them to learn how to walk, talk, and show emotions in socially appropriate ways (Heyes, 2009).

In fact, babies aren't the only ones to mimic body language. Adults, unconsciously and consciously, build rapport, communicate, and tune in emotionally to one another through behavioral mimicry (Thompson, 2012). Think of how hard it is to suppress the need to yawn when you witness someone in the act. Laughter, smiling, and even crying are contagious. It turns out that this emotional and behavioral contagion is the key not only to learning but also to survival (Thompson, 2012). This mechanism served our early ancestors well by helping them communicate and understand one another clearly. Mirror neurons also helped early humans to spread emotional arousal quickly in circumstances in which their safety was at risk (Molnar-Szakacs, Wu, Robles, & Iacoboni, 2007).

Mirror Neurons Activity

Dr. Shawn Achor is an American author and speaker, known for his work in the field of positive psychology at Harvard University. Achor's social experiments illustrate the importance of emotional contagion when considering positive culture in schools. You could easily incorporate the following seven-step activity into the first few minutes of a staff meeting, a morning meeting in a classroom, or even an assembly (Achor, 2010).

1. Have participants choose to sit or stand next to someone they don't normally work with.

2. Have each person in the partnership identify as either partner 1 or partner 2 using a creative method (such as hair length, eye color, birth month order, proximity to the exit sign, and so on). For example, the partner who is closest to the exit sign is partner 1, and the one farthest from the exit sign is partner 2.

3. Give the following instructions to partner 1: "Please draw on your years of self-discipline that have brought your to where you are at this point in your life. Your one and only job will be to remain emotionless during the next seven seconds, for the duration of what partner 2 will be asked to do to you. Please become emotionally neutral."

4. Give the following instructions to partner 2: "Smile the biggest, warmest, most genuine smile you can for the next seven seconds without breaking eye contact."

5. Have partners face each other. Make sure they are within striking distance of each other and that, for the next seven seconds, they maintain eye contact the entire time.

6. Have partners follow your instructions for seven seconds. When the time is up, invite partners to reflect on and discuss what they observed.

7. If you have time, have partners switch places so that partner 1 becomes the smiler and partner 2 becomes the receiver.

The setup to this activity is important. It builds emotional tension and simulates a stressful situation. Partner 1 has no idea what's about to happen. By the time I ask partners to face each other within striking distance, the pressure is high, eyes are wide, and many are questioning why they chose my workshop.

People do not like uncertainty. People do not like discomfort. Once folks realize the activity only asks them to defend themselves emotionally against a *smile*, the immediate relief is palpable. The partners get to work, and it's not long before you can see hands darting up to conceal smiles. Within seconds, the room is erupting with laughter.

We can see firsthand the contagious nature of laughter, and according to Achor (2010), this experiment yields a similar result in 80 to 85 percent of cases. This activity, while amusing and seemingly trivial, has the potential to shift culture in a massive way. It's a clear illustration of how easily we have the capacity to affect the general emotional climate within our environments, whether within the classroom, our school, or the broader community.

Happiness: The Antidote to Anxiety, Depression, and Loneliness

Happiness isn't the only contagious emotion (Achor, 2010). Sadness, anger, and frustration are also contagious. Kindness, it turns out, can serve as an antidote to many symptoms and emotions associated with depression, anxiety, and loneliness (Rowland, 2018). Depression and anxiety are on the rise in North America (World Health Organization, 2017). For example, between 2005 and 2015, depressive illness increased by approximately a fifth, according to the World Health Organization (World Health Organization, 2017). Depression is a treatable mental illness characterized by feelings of extreme sadness and low mood (ADAA, n.d.b).

These conditions of anxiety, depression, and loneliness are often worsened by our brain interpreting daily stressors and telling us that we're not safe, even when we're not in immediate danger (Sinek, 2014). When we're stressed, cortisol, a brain chemical, is released by the brain into our body (Nesse, Ellis, & Bhatnagar, 2016). It shuts down all nonessential functions in our bodies like digestion, growth, and the immune system so we can instantly react to danger by running away, fighting, or freezing (Sinek, 2014).

Sure, cortisol was a helpful chemical to keep us safe from saber-toothed tigers during the caveman days, but it is only meant to be in our bodies for short bursts (Sinek, 2014). When people feel stressed out more and more frequently, cortisol stays in their bodies way too long and can have harmful effects on their health and mental well-being.

Cortisol also directly stops the flow of oxytocin in the body (Li, Hassett, & Seng, 2018). Why is that such a big deal? Basically, it means that when we get stressed out, it's hard to feel love and empathy, and it's even harder to make connections to people. Here's where kindness has the power to make a change. Remember the love hormone, oxytocin? Researchers have found that when we engage in kindness, oxytocin is released and counteracts the cortisol in the body (Li et al., 2018).

Why Kindness Matters

Nearly one in five people in North America suffer from a diagnosed mental disorder in their lifetime, such as anxiety and depression (ADAA, n.d.a). Although we know we can't fix these problems, we do know that kindness has been proven to offset the negative effects of stress in our bodies (Sinek, 2009). It can also help us to build rapport and increase a sense of belonging within our schools (Brodrick, 2019). We have the power to make those around us feel seen and valued through generous acts and interactions, which can help them develop a sense of belonging and safety. These acts can be simple and cost-free, and can take only a few minutes to include within your daily routine.

Kindness Is Not Our Default Setting

Houston Kraft (2020), a world-renowned speaker and best-selling author about promoting kindness in schools, explains that people are often incapable of demonstrating generosity in the moment for five reasons: (1) incompetence, (2) inconvenience, (3) insecurity, (4) inconsistency, and (5) feeling too important. For examples of the ways these kindness roadblocks interfere with our ability to build community and create rapport, see table 4.2.

TABLE 4.2: FIVE ROADBLOCKS TO SHOWING KINDNESS

Reason	Description	Example
Incompetence	We don't always know how to respond when someone is struggling. We're worried we'll do it wrong. It's common to believe that our reaction could actually worsen the other person's state. So, often, we stay silent or choose not to reach out with the misguided belief that by saying nothing, we will do no harm. It turns out that the silence can be worse than a seemingly incompetent response. Sometimes, it's best to reach out even when we don't feel like we can *fix* a situation or when we don't feel like we have the right words.	Imagine that a colleague in your school has just lost her spouse due to an unexpected work-related accident. She is devastated. You feel helpless, but she's been on your mind a lot. Instead of calling her or reaching out, you decide to step back due to a belief that those who are closer to her should be the only ones to reach out and that you might just make it worse. Instead, you might want to send her a brief email or note to say that you're sorry for her loss. You might even choose to call her and admit that although you're not sure what to say, you want her to know that you're thinking of her.
Inconvenience	These days, our schedules are jammed with activities, events, lessons, birthday parties, get-togethers, book clubs, classes, and more. It can feel impossible to pause our own overwhelm in order to alleviate someone else's. Often, inconvenience can prevent us from showing kindness. Generous gestures don't have to be time-consuming; they can be as simple as adopting a kinder overall posture as you go to the grocery store or battle rush-hour traffic. It's amazing what a smile and wave can do for someone else.	You've been meaning to contribute to the holiday hamper collection for the family your school is sponsoring this year, but time has gotten away from you. You haven't had a chance to hand-pick a beautiful item to gift them and you might not make the deadline. Instead of agonizing over a perfect gift contribution, why not opt for an easy and convenient gift card?
Insecurity	People sometimes feel insecure about their ability to support one another. We might think, "Who am I to be the one to support someone though this?" Instead, it might be more helpful to think, "If not me, then who?" Sometimes kindness is a courageous act that pulls us from the comfort of our everyday routines into a place that challenges us to be even better people.	Picture that your administrator has just received difficult news from your district leaders about a challenging new measure they would like to implement. It will make work at school exceedingly challenging for the administrator due to increased data entry and tracking. Instead of feeling insecure, though these issues are likely beyond your pay grade, offer a listening ear. This kind gesture can help your administrator to feel a little less alone in his or her struggle.

continued →

Reason	Description	Example
Inconsistency	True kindness doesn't come from a checklist. While Kindness Weeks and Random Acts of Kindness are positive highlights in schools, workplaces, and communities, what we really need to do as a society is to focus on longevity and consistency when it comes to generosity, not simply a "one-and-done" approach. Part of our difficulty with expressing authentic kindness is that we often see it as an event instead of a set of character skills to be developed or an interactional posture we can adopt as a way of being.	Imagine that World Kindness Day is coming up and you decide to do a one-off activity about kindness. Your students feel excited about the activity for the day, but the next day, the theme of kindness is sidelined by other content that you need to get to. Instead of relying on one or two token days to focus on kindness in your classroom, reimagine ways to weave the theme of kindness into daily lessons and discussions as a way to promote longevity and consistency over time.
Feeling Too Important	I'd argue that most educators don't readily identify with this category, since we're a pretty giving bunch; however, many high-ranking CEOs or even some educational administrators might feel *too important* to show kindness and generosity to those they, either consciously or unconsciously, consider below them on the educational hierarchy. When we think of all the people who work within a school, it is worth reflecting on whether the staff's collective interactions reflect a culture of equity. Are the custodians, administrative assistants, educational assistants, and cafeteria workers treated with the same kindness as our classroom teachers and principals? How do the students tend to treat the school staff? Examining the day-to-day interactions we have in schools with one another can reveal a great deal about systemic inequities within them.	Every morning, the school custodian sweeps and mops the floors in your school building. When he makes conversation, he's noticed that certain colleagues in the school won't acknowledge him. While it's possible that they are simply too busy to make time for small talk, the custodian often senses that these individuals consider themselves too important to speak to him. Instead, we need to consider that everyone in our school building has an important role to play in keeping our learning space safe and functional, regardless of title and pay grade.

Source: Michael, 2019a.

Offering kindness is simple but not easy. Often, the stories we tell ourselves about our limitations can prevent us from being kind to others. We need to know that kindness can be normal in schools, an that although we may not understand or be able to fix the suffering of others, we can make a big impact through just one small act of being courageous enough to sit alongside someone and witness his or her suffering.

The Cost of Incivility

Being kind in a consistent way comes down to one guiding question: *Who* do you want to be? This is the question that Christine Porath, a tenured professor at Georgetown University's McDonough School of Business and author of *Mastering Civility: A Manifesto for the Workplace*, posed to a Nevada audience during her 2018 TED Talk. In this research-based talk, she offers unexpected insights about the price of rudeness in the workplace and how respectful behavior can increase your work success and your company's bottom line (Porath, 2018).

While it may seem that schools are dissimilar to corporate environments, many of Porath's findings are applicable to the educational setting. She argues that rudeness including gossip, mean-spirited texts, mocking and belittling, and general disrespect can result in lapses in judgement, loss in quality of performance, and chronic stress that can lead to health problems and even corresponding mortality in employees (Porath, 2018).

In a survey, Porath finds that incivility caused more than half of employees to reduce their productivity, 80 percent felt a sense of worry and stress, and more than 12 percent left their jobs altogether (Porath, 2016). One company reported that the effects of incivility within the company culture was costing over $12 million per year! In examining educator attrition, it's possible that hostile work environments contribute to decisions to leave the profession as well as correlating with heightened stress levels, depression, anxiety, and loneliness. When it comes to seeing these negative effects through the lens of an educator, it becomes clear that positive school culture is an essential component to overall educator well-being.

Furthermore, Porath (2016) finds that incivility was contagious and often resulted in toxic workplace cultures. Another study finds that even those witnessing rude interactions within the workplace experienced a decrease in productivity, which makes sense considering the neuroscience related to the contagion of emotion and the presence of mirror neurons. She explained, "Incivility is a bug. It's contagious, and we become carriers of it just by being around it. It affects our emotions, our motivation, our performance and how we treat others" (Porath, 2018).

Four Steps to Build Rapport With Anyone

So, how does one strike a balance between ambition and generosity? I turned to my friend David Knapp-Fisher, author and connection specialist. He hosts networking events and conferences for businesses and often shares his four easy tips for making the most of your interactions in order to live a meaningful, service-filled life. This framework also works well in a school-based setting (Michael, 2019b). Knapp-Fisher's four tips are as follows (Michael, 2019b).

1. **Greet:** When we engage with new people in our school building or our colleagues on a regular basis, it's important that we greet them. When it comes to social connections, we receive what we give. If we're friendly and act genuinely interested in what our colleagues, students, and parents have to say, chances are they'll feel the same way about us, or at least leave the interaction with a positive association with you. People generally love talking about their passions. We can invite them to do so while asking meaningful questions to demonstrate interest and build trust.

2. **Offer help:** Helping others doesn't mean making big offers of generosity, like helping a colleague on the weekend or babysitting our teaching partner's kids all the time. It can be as simple as offering the title of a helpful book we've read or forwarding a powerful podcast that aligns with another person's passion. Small acts make a big impact. We don't have to be completely selfless and lacking in boundaries to help people inch closer to their own goals, as Adam Grant points out in his 2013 book *Give and Take*, but helping them to do so can be mutually beneficial in the long run.

3. **Ask for support:** To nurture a reciprocal relationship, it's a good idea to ask others for help (Baker, 2014). Help-seeking can be challenging, especially for those of us who pride ourselves on being independent (Baker, 2014). Perhaps a colleague has expertise in something about which you need advice. Perhaps an educational assistant has planned a trip to place you've always wanted to go. It could be as simple as asking a colleague to give you feedback regarding the new report card format you're trialing this year. Reciprocity builds trust, and trust is the foundation for lasting relationships (Baker, 2014).

4. **Follow through:** Finally, as Knapp-Fisher asserts, follow-through is often the essential part of networking that people neglect (Michael, 2019b). Circle back! You may have had lofty ambitions to connect with someone in the future. Did you follow through? A quick email or check-in text can go a long way in solidifying your new connection and fostering a more long-lasting link.

How to build rapport with anyone is an important skill for educators to learn for success professionally but also to boost a sense of connection to the people with whom we work. It is especially important that we take into account our cultural blind spots as we aspire to create rapport with those who may have cultural contexts and backgrounds that differ from our own.

Cultural Blind Spots

Cultural blind spots can be damaging to the cohesion and inclusivity in our schools. Being aware of our limited perspectives and acknowledging our privilege is an important part of building inclusive, equitable school environments (Suarez-Orozco, et al., 2015). Imagine a class at lunchtime, eating alongside the classroom teacher. One of the girls in the class, a student who had immigrated from India a year earlier, has been eating rice. Suddenly, the teacher calls her name sharply, reprimanding her for eating the rice with her fingers. The teacher, unaware that it is customary for people of Indian heritage to eat rice with their dominant hand—a custom that reflects the belief that food is a sensory experience and the importance of touching the food prior to consumption to ensure that the temperature is appropriate—is imposing on the student the dominant Western ideology that food is eaten with utensils. Humiliated, the child takes a fork from the classroom fork jar and proceeds to eat her food in the only way the teacher considers acceptable.

This interaction is an example of a racialized microaggression, a systematic expression of racism and intolerance, and it is a direct result of white privilege and ignorance (DiAngelo, 2018). The teacher does not have the capacity to see beyond the blind spots of his own limited perspective. Reprimanding the child for the way she is eating is an attempt to assimilate her into the dominant colonial narrative about mealtimes and ultimately cast negative judgement on her culture's values and customs (DiAngelo, 2018). While it may not always be possible to guard against these blind spots, it's important to be open to the possibility that we might get it wrong and that there will be times when we need to repair mistakes we've made.

Most People Are Doing the Best They Can

It can be really challenging to make positive assumptions about others, especially if we are triggered into a fight, flight, or freeze response due to a difficult interaction. Just think about that student in your class who seems to act out at the most inopportune times, challenging your authority and hijacking your lessons. While you may know deep down that her interactions may be motivated by any combination of the emotional need for belonging, significance, and variety, there are times when it feels like a personal attack. It can take a great deal of patience to depersonalize those negative interactions.

It feels risky to be generous with our assumptions, especially when we interpret someone's intention as hurtful. If we view our interactions as zero sum, meaning that in order for someone to feel as though he or she has won, someone has to lose, that *someone* could be *us* (Smith, 2018). Altruism is not a zero-sum game; it's a win-win. Being in that state of mind, the risk of *losing* feels unpalatable. It may be much more desirable to take a side and fight for the win (Smith, 2018). This is often the point at which educators find themselves in a power struggle, grasping to regain control through empty threats or doling out illogical consequences. The mentality can become *win at all costs* (Smith, 2018). Casting people in a negative light is much easier than training ourselves to see the gray area and appealing to our own empathy to gain perspective (Smith, 2018). Creating a narrative of good versus bad is easy to do, especially when we feel threatened or when others sit alongside us with a rallying cry.

We spend so much of our time navigating our interactions with parents, students, and colleagues of diverse life experiences and perspectives so different from ours. Seeing those individuals through the lens of their intention ensures that we maximize our own happiness. What do I mean by *the lens of their intention*? Instead of trying to read between the lines, assuming the worst from people with whom we disagree, what if we truly believe that they are doing their best and that their intentions are motivated by a basic, unmet emotional need? What if we approach our conflicts not through the win-lose mentality but rather by asking ourselves, "What does this person *need* right now that I might be able to help him or her acquire?"

Belonging is a greater predictor of life expectancy, well-being, happiness, and fulfillment than heart health, poverty, smoking, or obesity (Achor, 2010). We are wired to seek out belonging through our connections to others. The mirror neurons in our bodies are designed to help us react and mimic the behaviors of those around us so we will belong more easily.

Our empathy, compassion, and acts of genuine kindness help us to show up for those around us in a benevolent manner that reinforces trust and respect. We are able to positively impact our own stress levels as well as those of others around us by engaging in meaningful interactions. Those meaningful interactions help us feel more connected to ourselves and those around us. They are essential to helping us feel fired up as educators, which is an important aspect of replenishing ourselves as individuals.

Strategies to Ignite Your Reconnecting Fire

In this section, you will explore actionable strategies for creating rapport within the school environment, tactics for counteracting toxic school-based culture, tangible ways of building trust and belonging in your school, and effective approaches to promote meaningful recognition. When you can practice social awareness and relationship skills, you will feel more well rounded and grounded as an educator. Contributing to a healthy school community not only benefits your students and colleagues; it also benefits you as a teacher.

Creating Rapport Strategies

What if it were possible to easily connect with anyone you meet—at educator conferences, at the photocopier, at the beginning of the school year, at parent-teacher conferences, and even at the local coffee shop? The following strategies—the EARS strategy and the What's in a Name? strategy—are techniques to help you build rapport with anyone.

The EARS Strategy

Brian Miller is a world-renowned corporate magician, the author of the best-selling book *Three New People*, a successful TED speaker (with 3.5 million views), and the podcast host of *Beyond Networking*. He offers the EARS strategy to develop meaningful connections and to show active listening within a conversation. This strategy is effective with your own adult interactions but is also a powerful framework to teach to your students in the classroom (Miller, 2018). Miller suggests building rapport through four steps.

1. **Making eye contact (E):** Practice giving a speaker or listener a comfortable level of eye contact.

2. **Avoiding distraction (A):** Stay focused on the person with whom you're talking—leave the phone alone!

3. **Reflecting back (R):** Reflect back to the speaker what he or she is saying in an authentic manner.

4. **Summarizing (S):** Always summarize the main points at the end of the interaction.

When you can show up for others without the need to insert your own responses and ideas into their message, you leave an interaction feeling seen and heard. As Stephen Covey (1989) asserts, you need to communicate with a desire to seek understanding, not to be understood yourself.

What's in a Name? Strategy

Names are an important conduit for creating a sense of trust and intimacy with someone, especially when used in a positive manner, because if there's one thing we love, it's hearing our own name. As educators, especially for those teaching preparatory classes or teaching in middle or secondary school, when hundreds of students pass through our classrooms, memorizing names can be an essential key to building a sense of belonging and cohesion within our classrooms. Also, it gives students a feeling of significance when teachers go out of their way to remember their names.

Huda Essa is an author, teacher, and social justice advocate, who asserts in her 2018 TED Talk that our names serve as symbols of our human cultural, environmental, and linguistic evolution. Names reflect beliefs, religious customs, familial traditions, and cultural structures. In Western cultures, those within minority groups whose names differ from the typical Western names often grow to dislike and even seek to change their names because of the immense pressure to conform and because of racism and unconscious bias (Essa, 2018). Sometimes, teachers will simply avoid mispronouncing unfamiliar names by not ever saying a student's name because they don't want to get it wrong, to the detriment of the student, their relationship, and the class as a whole (Essa, 2018). We can learn a great deal about our names; names serve as the key that unlocks a deep intercultural understanding (Essa, 2018).

Review figure 4.1 for multisensory tips to remember anyone's name, whether you are in the classroom, at a networking function, or with your colleagues.

Strategy	*Description*	*Example*
Spell It	One of the easiest ways to remember someone's name is to ask him or her to spell it. Spelling a name out allows you to visualize it, which anchors it in the visual memory centers of your brain (Miller, 2018).	Tricky names: *"How is that spelled?"* *"M-o-r-g-a-n-e."* Common names: *We can ask "Jeff" whether it's spelled with a G or a J.*
Repeat It	Within the first five to ten seconds, make it your mission to repeat the name a minimum of three times. Although it sounds strange and scripted to us when we do this, the recipient tends to enjoy hearing his or her name so much that it doesn't even seem as strange that someone would say it three times in such rapid succession (Miller, 2018).	*"Hi Ashley. It's nice to meet you, Ashley. What's your favorite subject in school, Ashley?"*
Alliterate It	In your mind, as you are being introduced to the individual whose name you'd like to remember, choose an adjective or memorable word that begins with the same letter as the person's name. Better yet, connect a visual image to the word to anchor the name in your memory (Miller, 2018).	• *Mighty Miles* • *Wacky Wanda* • *Cashier Carly* • *Tiny Tina* • *Funny Fiona*
Build and Return	Greeting students at the door is a favorite way to build positivity into the morning, but David Jay (aka The Dope Educator) takes it to the next level. Throughout his day, he greets every single one of his seventy-five middle school students by name and by their personalized handshake. He memorizes each handshake with this build and return approach (Michael, 2019f).	How to learn multiple names and handshakes: 1. Every student thinks of a handshake with no more than three moves. 2. Learn the handshakes for five students at a time. 3. Move to the next five students, then return and review the first five students' handshakes. 4. Continue learning and reviewing the names and handshakes until you've made it through the class. 5. Repeat the following day.

Figure 4.1: Strategies for remembering names.   *continued →*

Strategy	Description	Example
Teach Us Your Name	Instead of avoiding the names that seem different than the dominant cultural happenstance, Essa (2018) suggests having students teach you their names explicitly, delving into the history, culture, and linguistic origin of their names for the mutual benefit of all involved.	1. Invite the individual to teach you his or her name: "Can you teach me your name?" 2. Ask, "How is your name pronounced?" Ask the individual to pronounce his or her name slowly. 3. Repeat the name, syllable by syllable. 4. You may want to write the name down or connect it to a known word. 5. If it is helpful, relevant, and respectful, you may ask to learn more about the origin of the individual's name related to his or her cultural history. It can deepen your understanding of the individual and your relationship.

Learning names and building immediate rapport is important as we get to know one another within our classrooms and schools, but trust is also about intentional ongoing leadership practices and approaches that enable those within our institutions to feel valued and seen. Research finds, "Creating an effective learning climate often includes making students feel recognized as individuals, both by instructors and by peers" (Ambrose, Bridges, DiPietro, Lovett, & Norman, 2010, p. 182). Learning your students' names and facilitating an opportunity for students to learn one another's names fosters a sense of community and decreases anonymity (Ambrose et al., 2010).

Strategies for Counteracting Toxic School Culture

The following strategy can help you counteract a toxic school culture in both the staff and student populations.

21 Days of Kindness Challenge Activity

It has been said that it can take as little as twenty-one days to build the foundation for a new habit and around sixty-six to entrench the habit longer-term (Gardner, Lally, & Wardle, 2012). Why not launch a whole-school 21 Days of Kindness Challenge in your school to jump-start a culture of kindness?

Staff Challenge

An easy way to launch a kindness challenge is to post a bingo board on your staffroom wall with twenty-one kindness challenges printed within a large grid. The staff at your school can sign their names beside each one they complete, or each staff member can keep a personalized photocopied version handy. Each time people complete one of the challenges, they can put an X through one of the squares. Whoever manages to complete the most challenges within an agreed-on time frame wins the challenge. It could be fun to have some prizes for first, second, and third place!

Here are some ideas to include on your 21 Days of Kindness bingo board.

- Buy a colleague a coffee.
- Offer to teach a colleague's gym class or take his or her students for an extra thirty minutes.
- Go outside with a buddy class and do garbage clean-up (make it a friendly competition with another buddy class).
- Text five teacher friends a lovely morning message to brighten their day.
- Offer to carry a fellow teacher's materials on the way into school.
- Plan a Friday after-school visit.
- Plan an after-school exercise date.
- Walk at lunch with a few colleagues (invite some people with whom you wouldn't normally spend time).
- Write notes of gratitude for the support staff in your school.
- Leave a secret gift for a different colleague each day.
- Buy some treats for the staff room.

Student Challenge

With students, you might want to launch a structured kindness inquiry, asking the students, "How can we be kind?" Students can brainstorm a different act of kindness for every day of the twenty-one-day duration. The ideas could be placed on a class calendar or pulled from a hat. There are truly so many ways to adapt the challenge for any level, interest, and classroom theme. Running the 21-Day Kindness Challenge throughout the school as a whole is a powerful way to effect positive change and to reinforce common values.

Play Together!

It can be easy to get carried away with the stresses of everyday school life. One way to counteract stressful or even toxic school culture is to plan regular ways of engaging creatively or socially together. In my experience, some of the most positive school cultures were born from our time spent together outside of the classroom.

A memorable Christmas tradition at Sir James Douglas School in Victoria, BC, where I first started my career in a kindergarten class, was the *Nom de Plume* Annual Breakfast. On the last day before winter break, our entire staff (teachers, administrators, custodians, and educational assistants) would gather in the school staff room at 7:30 a.m. to celebrate together. Everyone would bring something delicious to share—there was always an impressive breakfast spread with homemade quiche, bread, casseroles, bacon, sausage, eggs, fresh-squeezed juices, French toast, hot chocolate, and gourmet coffee. Then, once everyone had served themselves, we would sit together and start our *Nom de Plume* Ceremony.

In the weeks leading up to this special annual event, Trish Robinson, our staff's resident organizer extraordinaire (who taught first grade down the hall from me), would have every member on staff think of a *nom de plume* for themselves—a pen name that would represent them symbolically—and put the names in a hat. For example, one year, since I love to bake and decorate cupcakes, I called myself the Cupcake Queen. Someone else used the coordinates to his birthplace in Sweden as his *nom de plume*. Another colleague called herself the Poem Master, since it was her favorite subject to teach.

Prior to the breakfast, each attendee was responsible for purchasing a small, inexpensive gift. Usually the gifts were hilarious; sometimes they were sentimental. Some of us wrote songs, jokes, poems, or letters. The creativity that came out of our staff was awe-inspiring. At the breakfast, everyone on staff would pick a name from the hat, then would try to guess who their chosen person was based on their cryptic *nom de plume*. My favorite part of the whole morning was watching as people presented their gifts to their chosen *nom de plume*. There were often tears, hugs, and a ton of laughter, especially when our guesses were off the mark completely. This annual ritual made our staff strong. These moments and memories glued us together whenever things became challenging in our staff meetings or with our students. We saw each other as people first.

How might your staff be able to adopt new, positive rituals to strengthen your staff cohesion and collaboration? What are some playful ways that your staff and colleagues might be able to build strong connection and trust? Explore some of the following ideas and plan an activity with your staff.

- Hold an annual year-end themed, dress-up barbecue.

- Plan a citywide scavenger hunt in teams.

- Join a local community fundraiser and volunteer as a staff member.

- Host a staff lunchtime soup club once per month.

- Celebrate individual staff members on their special day by assigning birthday buddies.

Strategies for Building Trust and Fostering Belonging

Trust is an integral part of our success as educators (Mineo, 2014). The way in which you interact with your colleagues, your students, and the parents of the students in your classes either builds or breaks trust. When your students trust you, you can teach them effectively. When you can reach and teach your students, it makes you feel empowered and effective (Yin, Chi-Kin, Lee, Jin, & Zhang, 2012). Fostering a sense of trust and belonging in the classroom is deeply connected to your own sense of efficacy and well-being as an educator.

The Marble Jar Activity

Within the classroom, a jar of marbles can illustrate trust. Brené Brown (2015) writes about this idea in her book *Rising Strong*. Brown, a researcher-storyteller and professor at the University of Houston, has become well known through her extensive body of work on shame and vulnerability. In her book *Daring Greatly*, she states that "vulnerability is about sharing our feelings and our experiences with people who have earned the right to hear them. Being vulnerable and open is mutual and an integral part of the trust-building process" (Brown, 2012, p. 45). Therefore, vulnerability is an important component of trust building because it showcases an element of common humanity—the idea that we're all in this together, and it is the foundation for the marble jar illustration of trust.

To introduce the marble jar activity, use the following five-step instructions.

1. Ask the class to imagine that the trust in each of the relationships in their lives is represented by a jar that can be filled with marbles. Show the class a medium-sized jar and a large sack of marbles.

2. Explain that we can deposit marbles and accumulate our sense of trust or withdraw them and degrade that sense of trust through our interactions.

    a. As a class, create a list of the things that tend to contribute to trust individually and as a class. For example, when a student helps another student who is hurt, the first student is showing trustworthy behavior. When the class returns quickly from a recess break, they have earned the teacher's trust.

    b. Create a list of ways that we can degrade a sense of trust as individuals or as a class. For example, leaving others out of a game or activity can erode trust with them. When a student takes supplies from the teacher's desk without asking, that behavior can make it hard for the teacher to trust the whole class.

3. When someone makes more deposits than withdrawals, generally, we tend to put our trust in that person.

4. Using the marble jar, take note when individuals and the class as a whole contribute to the feeling of trust in the classroom or take away from it. Place the marbles in the jar and remove them, accordingly, with the goal of filling the jar.

5. Have each student create his or her own paper version of the marble jar. Invite students to make note of things that fill and empty their jars that relate to friendships and interactions.

Brown (2015) explains that trust can be deposited through any of the following.

- Asking for help
- Receiving the generosity of others
- Giving without recompense
- Offering meaningful feedback
- Establishing clear boundaries
- Demonstrating capability
- Taking responsibility for your actions
- Keeping your word
- Demonstrating integrity

- Being courageous around others

- Assuming the best of people

Trust is built in the micro-moments, the seemingly insignificant moments of interaction (Brown, 2015). Developing trust within your classroom and school culture is an essential aspect of promoting the well-being of those within your school. While this activity is geared specifically toward the way you might approach trust-building in your classroom, it is applicable to your broader relationships with your colleagues, administrators, paraprofessionals, and even family members.

The Circle of Safety Activity

When starting the year, it is always an educator's goal to establish an environment of psychological safety and trust within the classroom and contribute to a broader atmosphere of safety within the school. In his book *Leaders Eat Last* (2014), Simon Sinek uses the term *circle of safety* to describe the ideal conditions we want to establish within any organization that enable a culture of trust, belonging, and psychological safety to exist. The circle of safety envelops an entire organization, not just a limited few who have a title of authority attached to their name, and it provides the ideal conditions for learning, innovation, creativity, and self-expression (Sinek, 2014). This activity could be adapted to create a staff vision for the school culture and community. Here are four steps for how to facilitate the circle of safety in your classroom.

1. Establish a shared vision for the classroom based on respectful behaviors. What kind of classroom do we wish to have? What will we see? What will it sound like? What will we hear? What will it feel like? For example, *We want a classroom where we all feel respected. We will see smiling, walking, sharing, and cooperation. We will hear kind words, creative ideas, and encouraging, respectful language. We will feel brave, happy, and calm.*

2. Write a class promise based on the type of classroom you wish to have. For example, *We promise to be kind, to try our best, and to be safe in our environment, with each other, and for ourselves.*

3. Have students sign the promise.

4. Refer to the promise throughout the year, reminding students of their shared vision for a happy, learning classroom.

Within the circle of safety, you can access the full potential of your neo-cortex because you do not feel threatened or triggered emotionally (Sinek, 2014). Part of establishing a psychologically safe learning environment comes from building trust.

The Seven-Day Text Challenge Activity

Remember the "three good things" activity from chapter 1 (page 27)? For this activity created by Lisa Baylis, a school counsellor, Mindfulness for Educators instructor, and the author of *Self-Compassion for Educators*, we'll throw in one part gratitude and one part friendship for an ideal *connection* cocktail (Michael, 2018b). Here's how it works in six steps.

1. Choose an educator friend or colleague with whom to do this challenge for one week.

2. Dedicate three to five minutes each evening to reflect on one good thing that happened to you that day.

3. Text your friend about your gratitude. For example, *Today I managed to check off my list of things to do during my thirty-minute prep period!*

4. Celebrate your colleague's gratitude and the fact that even just for a moment, you've had a chance to connect meaningfully with someone important in your life.

5. Repeat the process throughout the week.

6. At the end of the week, reflect about your overall feelings toward your friend, yourself, and your overall happiness.

Strategy for Facilitating Meaningful Recognition

As an educator, you provide positive and constructive feedback to students, colleagues, and administrators on a regular basis. How you give feedback can affect your relationships, positively and negatively. According to relationship researcher John Gottman, there exists a proven ratio of authentic positive to negative interactions within positive relationships (Benson, 2017). He states that for every negative interaction between individuals, there must be five positive subsequent interactions to maintain the health of the relationship. In other words, "unless positive interactions outnumber negative interactions by five to one, odds are that the relationship will fail" (Benson, 2017).

Two-by-Ten Activity

The following two-step activity is an approach called the *two by ten*, which works well to increase authentic opportunities for positive interactions (McKibben, 2014).

1. Choose a student who tends to be particularly high-profile within your classroom, who tends to require significant and frequent constructive feedback throughout the day. For example, focus on a disruptive student who struggles to be respectful within the classroom.

2. Set aside two minutes throughout the day to connect with the student in a positive way for the next ten days. Compliment him or her on something he or she is doing well. Share a joke. Talk about his or her interests. Show curiosity about his or her pastimes by asking authentic, meaningful questions.

What if we could be a little more aware of interactions, keeping Gottman's rule in mind as we do so? How might our classrooms cultures be different? How might we feel knowing that most of our interactions were positive? We all know that successful educators are effective because of the relationships they build. Increasing our positive interactions may not always reap immediate rewards; however, it does contribute to a happier classroom environment and, therefore, a happier teacher.

Conclusion

In this chapter, we have explored how to connect more meaningfully to those around us as a means of becoming happier and contributing to the positive culture in our schools. We have examined the science of generosity, exploring the physiological and morale-building benefits of kindness. Through exploring relevant research related to fostering trust, vulnerability, perspective-taking, and recognition, we've explored ways to contribute to a more positive school culture.

In reading this chapter, I hope you come away excited and inspired to nurture your current relationships and to establish a strong foundation for future relationships. I have confidence that you will feel empowered by the fact that generosity can be the key to workplace happiness and to use that empowerment to push against a taker culture. We should be lifting one another up, recognizing and celebrating the accomplishments of others, and operating from a standpoint of abundance, with the knowledge that success and happiness is not a scarce resource. Connection begets connection. All of us are hardwired for human connection, and making connection a priority is essential to becoming a fired-up educator.

REVEAL

Your True Self:
How to Embrace Creativity as an
Expression of Your Humanity

*Stop asking for permission. Stop waiting to be picked. Reject
the tyranny of "picked." Pick yourself.*

—Seth Godin

Creativity is accessible to everyone. Yes, you can embrace your own creativity! We all have the capacity to be creative, but we need to be courageous enough to allow it into our lives and habitual practice. When we allow ourselves the experience of being creative, without the expectation of outcome, we tap into energy that is bigger than ourselves, the very essence of humanity; we have the capacity to solve some of the most complicated problems that exist; and we learn to be the fullest expressions of ourselves. My experience is that practicing creativity can connect us to a deeper sense of well-being and purpose.

In this chapter, you will explore what the research says about our innate gift of—and need to express—creativity. You will learn how creativity typically declines with age, and how you can combat that by including opportunities for creativity in your daily life. You will discover the benefits of creativity to both educators and students and explore typical roadblocks to creativity. This chapter concludes with strategies to foster a creative mindset and establish a strong creative practice.

What the Research Says About Revealing Creativity

Creativity is an underrated but essential capacity that educators should work intentionally to develop within their students as well as within themselves, professionally and personally, to promote well-being, self-efficacy, and a sense of happiness (Diaz-Varela & Wright, 2019). People with high levels of social-emotional competence tend to show high corresponding levels of creativity (Gotlieb, Jahner, Immordino-Yang, & Kaufman, 2016). Creativity is closely tied to social-emotional competence and helps us to be successful in our jobs and within our personal lives (Fishman-Weaver, 2019). When we combine our social-emotional skills in self-awareness, self-management, social awareness, relationship building, and responsible decision-making, we can tap into our creativity in a more profound way, leading to more authentic self-expression (Fishman-Weaver, 2019).

The Decline in Our Creativity Over Time

At some point as adults, many of us grow out of our creativity practice. Author Carlton Noyes remarked in his 1907 book *The Gate of Appreciation*, "The child is the first artist. Out of the material around him he creates a world of his own . . . . His play is his expression" (p. 29). As we grow into adulthood, the burden of responsibilities can cause our playful creativity to wane. Jarvis (2019) states that "as adults, the chronic stress and uncertainty of modern life keep us in that closed place, focused on checking off the next box on our to-do list" (p. 10). Researchers have found that when it comes to creativity, only 25 percent of people believe that they are living up to their potential (Kelley & Kelley, 2013). Additionally, shaming incidents related to creativity can cause profound losses in creative confidence that can carry over into adulthood. For example, children may feel ashamed of their creativity if a teacher or fellow student degrades a drawing they've spent a great deal of effort making or a piece of writing they feel proud to have written. As Kelley and Kelley (2013) assert, "When a child loses the confidence to be creative, the impact can be profound" (p. 55).

Divergent thinking—finding creative solutions to problems—peaks in childhood and often dramatically tapers off in adulthood (Gopnik et al., 2017), so if we want to create the potential for future generations to hold onto their creative abilities into their adulthood, it is essential that educators work diligently to support students through their own creative journey in school while modelling a resilient and strong creative practice themselves. We can teach ourselves to be creative thinkers (Kelley & Kelley, 2013). We can relearn the art of being creative as adults, and we should, because our well-being depends on it! Divergent thinking is an important quality in educators, specifically, because it helps us to solve problems, think outside of the box, and create worthwhile learning opportunities for our students.

We Are All Creative

We are all born creative. Most typical kindergarteners can imagine a complex make-believe world using just a few props and suspension of disbelief. Authors and creative thought leaders Tom Kelley and David Kelley (2013) state in their book *Creative Confidence*, "Our fear of being judged is something we learn at a young age. But we don't start out with it. Most children are naturally daring" (p. 53). Any young child can take an empty yogurt container into the bath and subsequently lose themselves in an elaborate story of pirate ships, high seas, and lost treasure. According to Chase Jarvis (2019), author and world-renowned professional photographer, "Creativity is the practice of combining or rearranging two or more things in new and useful ways" (p. 8).

Creativity isn't simply reserved for working artists; it is a way of life, Jarvis asserts. He states, "Yes, art is a subset of creativity, but creativity [is] . . . the ability to make your ideas manifest in the world" (Jarvis, 2019, p. 10). Creativity can be expressed through the way we prepare our meals, the hobbies we take up in the lunchroom to pass the time, the way we decorate our classrooms at the beginning of the year, our approach to problem solving in the classroom, and even the way we craft our report card comments. It is a fallacy that the world is divided into creative and noncreative people. Creativity is the way that we pour our heart and soul into all that we do, whether in our role as teachers or in our personal lives. Creativity is everywhere; however, it can be difficult to access as we grow into adulthood.

Despite our busy adult lives, there are ways we can incorporate creativity on a daily basis. Bea Keizers is an elementary school educational assistant and Hebrew school teacher. Spinning, weaving, knitting, and crochet have been significant parts of Bea's life since she first learned the skills from her mother and grandmother as a young girl. A bright child, Bea always finished her schoolwork early, and she fondly remembers her third-grade teacher Mrs. Mitchell allowing her to crochet at her desk, as long as she was quiet about it. "I always had my hands in fiber," she told me (B. Keizers, personal communication, June 18, 2021).

As an adult, working with a variety of exceptional children with special needs and planning lessons for extracurricular Hebrew school, she takes time every morning to do a few rows of knitting or crochet as a means of feeding her soul before she arrives at work for a busy day. "Something about the quiet stillness of yarn work, the repetitive action, brings me peace before the frantic pace of the day," she said (B. Keizers, personal communication, June 18, 2021). Moreover, the act of creating something tangible gives her a sense of accomplishment and competence. As educators, solving day-to-day challenges with our students, both abstract and tangible, can leave us feeling depleted and ineffective. "I can come home and weave two inches of a complicated loom and say, *that much* I did today," Bea asserts.

Several years ago, while Bea was supporting a child during a physical education badminton lesson, an accident left her with a broken arm and severe brain trauma. After the accident, she was unable to speak English and could only converse in German (her first language). She also experienced difficulty with sequencing and processing, key skills for her yarn-based crafts. "This period in my life gave me great compassion for brain diversity," she remembers. "Maybe I had grown smug, but this showed me how quickly it could all go away. I couldn't knit or weave anymore" (B. Keizers, personal communication, June 18, 2021).

Day by day, Bea regained the use of her arm and relearned English. What amazed her doctors most, however, was how weaving, knitting, and crocheting served as the conduit for her brain rehabilitation. Bea was diligent about her craft. It had been her lifeline as a child, but now it became the way in which she was able to regain a sense of self-expression. She continues to support children as an educational assistant in my school and makes a remarkable difference in their lives every day.

To read about additional examples of creative educators, scan the QR code on this page.

The Benefit of Creativity in School and Our Global World

Our purpose as educators during the 21st century, most of us would agree, is to prepare those within our charge for the unpredictable future (Moran, 2018). In schools, there are a variety of possible approaches for preparing students, but our ability to help them develop their imagination and capacity for creativity is especially important (Moran, 2018). When we can be creative, we can see the potential for growth, innovation, and development. Without creativity, we can't adapt in a modern, ever-changing world. In his highly viewed 2006 TED Talk, *Do Schools Kill Creativity?,* the late Sir Ken Robinson famously asserts that creativity should be considered one of the most important competencies that students can gain in school and that it is just as important as literacy instruction. Creativity needs to be at the forefront of our curriculum and embedded into our own way of life as educators.

According to best-selling author Seth Godin (2012), effective educators prepare their students for the future by teaching their students to solve *interesting* problems and by developing the *leader* within each of them. Effective problem solving and leadership require creativity, flexibility, an ability to stretch beyond our point of view by taking on other perspectives, and a capacity for connecting the dots (Godin, 2012). Creativity allows us to leap beyond the status quo and imagine a new, improved possibility for the future.

Inquiry-based approaches in the classroom have been popularized as ways to reinforce student-led learning by showcasing and exploring individual curiosities and play (MacKenzie & Bathurst-Hunt, 2019). Inquiry allows students to express themselves as individuals, while teaching them how to pursue their own passions and curiosities. According to co-authors Trevor MacKenzie and Rebecca Bathurst-Hunt (2019), successful inquiry-based classrooms have teachers who have become intimately connected to their own inquiry mindset and pursuits. Effective teachers have also learned how to harness their own curiosity and model essential characteristics, such as play, creativity, passion, and an ability to *go outside to come back in* that helps them to be authentic, curious learners, professionally and personally. Sometimes, it's important to step outside of our comfort zone and area of expertise, to learn new things through new experiences, then bring that knowledge, experience, and newfound passion back into the classroom; this is the true essence of *going outside to come back in.*

Curiosity is an essential component of a creative, inquiry-based classroom because the teacher "cultivates their students' curiosity through provocations and wonderings, modelling how inquisitive questions can drive learning opportunities" (MacKenzie & Bathurst-Hunt, 2019, p. 6). Play is an important focus for any creative educator, whereby they "see challenges as opportunities to tinker in their practice and look at problems from different angles" (MacKenzie & Bathurst-Hunt, 2019, p. 3). Although most of the research in play-based learning focuses on children, a recent focus on research related to teacher playfulness and play-based learning within the context of teacher training is emerging and points to mutual benefits for teachers and students (Diaz-Varela & Wright, 2019). Researchers have discovered the essential value of play in teacher education and highlighted the positive effects for student and teacher learning, as well as increased social-emotional competence in both students and teachers (Diaz-Varela & Wright, 2019). Teachers of inquiry-based methods are passionate, finding "joy in learning and doing, and [sharing] their delight with others" (MacKenzie & Bathurst-Hunt, 2019, p. 3).

Teachers of inquiry-based methods are able to look outside of their classroom and perspective to gain a fresh point of view about a topic or concept. Often, going outside to come back in results in helpful cross-pollination of ideas. The concept of *20-percent time* in classrooms is an opportunity for students to explore passion or inquiry-based projects for 20 percent of their day or week as a practice in promoting student agency in their own learning journeys. It was born from examining the value of the creative culture at Google and applying this culture to education (Juliani, 2013). At Google, employees are given 20 percent of their allocated work time to dedicate to something beyond their current assignment through the company (Juliani, 2013). As it turns out, a focus on creativity in the classroom doesn't just benefit our students; it also directly benefits educators on a professional and personal level.

The Personal Benefit of Creativity for Educators

As educators, we should aspire to tap into our creativity within our professional domain for the benefit of our students. Creativity is a conduit through which to express our lived experiences as educators, and it enrichens our personal lives as well as those of our students. When it comes to overwhelm and feeling burnt out as educators, playfulness and curiosity can serve as a welcome antidote. Creativity and play cause several well-documented benefits, including boosting happiness, improving overall mental wellness, and helping to strengthen the neural pathways in our brains (Kelley & Kelley, 2013).

Boosting Happiness

Engaging in creative activities that make us feel competent and calm (for example, sewing, drawing, crocheting, reconfiguring our classroom layout, drawing, or writing) activates flow. Creativity is rooted in flow, which psychologist, speaker, and author Mihaly Csikszentmihalyi (2004) states is essential to our human expression of purpose and meaning. Csikszentmihalyi has made it his life's work to find out what makes people happy and deeply fulfilled. In his 2004 TED Talk, *The Secret to Happiness*, he explores the fact that material goods do not ensure happiness, and that true happiness is found when one is in *flow*. Most humans can connect to an activity that puts us into flow. Flow is play and a true expression of creativity. Just the act of completing a task floods our brain with dopamine, which makes us feel good and connects us to the reward circuitry in our brain, helping us to feel accomplished and proud of ourselves (Stahl, 2018).

Improving Mental Wellness

Creativity and divergent thinking can contribute to a sense of mental wellness and can dramatically reduce depression, anxiety, and loneliness in people (Stahl, 2018). Expressive writing has been found to be especially helpful for regulating our mental health (Cohut, 2018). Some of my happiest memories, when I felt the most connected to myself on a deep, spiritual level, have been when I was singing with friends around a campfire, writing for my blog, planning and collaborating new units with colleagues, or decorating a cake for my child's birthday. Little moments of creativity can leave one feeling wholehearted and happy. Making space and time to appreciate the significance of these moments in our overall sense of well-being helps us to reap the benefits of our own creativity.

Strengthening Our Brains

Creativity can play a role in stimulating the connection between the left and right hemispheres of our brain, creating multiple neural pathways that enable us to be more flexible and creative (Vitale, 2011). According to research, despite a common understanding that analytical people (like mathematicians) are left-brained while more creative people (like musicians) are considered right-brained, we are learning that many musicians and artists marry the analytical and creative traits within the two brains (Vitale, 2011). Essentially, creativity and art can make us *smarter*!

Creativity is what helps us to identify and solve challenging problems. It helps us bring a sense of meaning and purpose to the world. Learning to lean into our creativity makes us better educators, but it also makes us happier, more wholehearted individuals.

Creative Roadblocks

So, where does all that imagination and creative thinking *go* when we grow into adults? There are a few factors that have the potential to limit our creative confidence, including time confetti (the fettering away of valuable time on trivial, time-eating tasks), procrastination, perfectionism, and comparison, as well as playing small (keeping our dreams small and realistic as opposed to shooting for the stars) in psychologically unsafe work, learning, and living spaces.

Time Confetti

Time confetti, a term coined by Brigid Schulte (2014) in her book *Overwhelmed: Work, Love, and Play When No One Has the Time*, refers to the incremental, frequent, and seemingly insignificant moments of time lost daily as a result of ineffective multitasking and tech-related interruptions. These days, we have more leisure time than our predecessors did just fifty years ago, according to Ashley Whillans (2020), author of *Time Smart: How to Reclaim Your Time and Live a Happier Life*. She says that despite this fact, we are still *time poor* as a result of technology, increased responsibilities, and the blurring of lines between work and home. As educators, we see this line grow even more faint as our assessment practices, communication with parents and colleagues, and even teaching itself have moved to online platforms. We also are allowing the prevalence and ubiquity of technological devices to interrupt our efforts to be creative. Because being creative is hard work, the resistance will turn to anything to interrupt flow (Seppälä, 2017). Unfortunately, our devices have been designed to capitalize on our brain's reward center and make this resistance easy by encouraging us to keep checking and rechecking our social media channels for notifications (Seppälä, 2017).

Social media companies employ the same strategies used by casinos, which activate the same brain mechanisms as highly addictive drugs such as cocaine (Matei, 2019). It's no wonder we're addicted to our technology. According to statistics gathered by the RescueTime application, "the top 20% of smartphone users spend more than 4.5 hours a day on their phones" (MacKay, 2019). When we extrapolate those numbers, those hours add up to some serious time: it equates to sixty-eight full days per year of time on technology. What could you do instead in sixty-eight days? Finish those scrapbooks from the past ten years of photos? Read thirty books? Create a business to earn extra income? Start writing a book? Plan new detailed units for the next few years? Exercise consistently? Learn a new skill? Meet new people? Start a book club? Take a bunch of courses? There are endless ways that we can reclaim our lost time in such a way that it benefits us!

If you want to be creative, you need to create boundaries for yourself that nothing can infiltrate to derail your creative expression. For example, consider the following boundaries.

- Decide on a specific time to be creative, when you can turn off the TV and disconnect from your phone.

- Turn off your email notifications on your desktop.

- Leave the phone alone when you're out with a friend or family member.

- Dedicate time (a few hours or even a whole day) for being tech-free.

- Get comfortable with the quiet and get to work!

Procrastination

Creativity begets creativity, while procrastination gets in the way of free-flowing, generative creativity. To get good ideas, you must suffer through a lot of bad ones (Kelley & Kelley, 2013), but procrastination can interrupt that process entirely. Procrastination is paralysis that prevents us from propelling ourselves from where we *are* to where we know we ought to *be*. As researchers Jeffrey Pfeffer and Robert Sutton (1999) note in their book *The Knowing-Doing Gap*, there is a gap between *knowing* and *doing* that prevents us from acting when we are fearful of our lack of ability or the outcome of the action. We can *decide* to become creative; creativity is not simply something that just *happens* to us. As professors and brothers Tom Kelley and David Kelley (2013) assert, "You need to deliberately choose creativity" (p. 76). You must make yourself open to creativity. The key to generating a creative mindset is to get used to the act of producing creatively, which means that you have to carve out the time and desire to do so, in spite of the discomfort (Jarvis, 2019).

Sometimes, procrastination can prevent us from even getting started on a creative task. We can feel stuck, overcome by a general creative version of writer's block. As author Seth Godin told me in an interview on *KindSight 101*, "There's no such thing as writer's block" (as cited in Michael, 2018f). Instead, he asserts, procrastination is just a form of fear that we need to confront if we want to be professionals and do work that matters. Procrastination is a manifestation of becoming overwhelmed by how big something feels and putting it off for as long as possible to avoid the discomfort that comes when we learn new things.

In her book *Bird by Bird*, author Anne Lamott (1995) tells the story of her then ten-year-old brother's process of writing a dreaded book report on birds. It was the night before the report was due, and her brother had not started writing it. Sitting beside her exasperated brother, Lamott's father explained that all his son needed to do was focus on the report by writing about one single bird at a time— *bird by bird*. As a writer, Lamott uses the same philosophy to overcome fear-based procrastination in her creative ventures. Often, we can become overwhelmed by the grandiosity of a task. Our students, too, can feel overwhelmed by their assignments. Instead, chunking it into small, manageable bits can make any creative task more achievable and less daunting.

Perfectionism

Perfectionism is the enemy of creativity because it inserts doubt and fear into our vulnerable self-expression before we even get started. In her book *Big Magic*, Elizabeth Gilbert (2015) asserts, "I think perfectionism is just a high-end, haute-couture version of fear. . . . Because underneath that shiny veneer, perfectionism is nothing more than a deep existential angst that says, again and again, 'I am not good enough and I will never be good enough'" (p. 167). Perfectionism prevents us from allowing for the important iterative risk taking to occur when we are innovating and experimenting in our professional and personal lives. Often, the "desire to be best gets in the way of getting better" (Kelley & Kelley, 2013, p. 122).

When we think of our work as educators, we can challenge ourselves to create a variety of lessons and units about a topic. The practice of creating and re-creating learning opportunities allows for tweaking and playfulness in our planning.

Comparison

Related to perfectionism is its evil twin, comparison. Whether we are scrolling social media, browsing online crafting sites, or walking the hallways of our schools, it's hard not to compare ourselves to the highlight reel displayed by other educators. According to psychologists, 10 percent of our thoughts are consumed by comparison (Summerville, 2019). Comparison generally doesn't feel good, especially if we are comparing ourselves to someone in a seemingly better circumstance (Summerville, 2019). The act of comparison can rob us of our originality and the very magic that makes us unique.

As Kelley and Kelley state in their book *Creative Confidence* (2013), "If you're concerned about conforming or about how you measure up to others' successes, you won't perform the risk-taking and trailblazing inherent in creative endeavors" (p. 57). In other words, comparison prevents us from actively embracing our capacity for creative expression. It also makes us feel badly about ourselves. To overcome the negative effects of comparison, we need to stop looking over our shoulders for confirmation that we are not good enough, and tune back into what makes us come alive.

Psychologically Unsafe Environments and Playing Small

Developing psychological safety is important in SEL (CASEL, 2020). According to a *Harvard Business Review* article by Laura Delizonna (2017), psychological safety "allows for moderate risk-taking, speaking your mind, creativity, and sticking your neck out without fear of having it cut off" and that it is essential for creating trust and success in organizations. In order to take the necessary risks involved in learning, one has to feel safe within the learning space.

The fear of social rejection can keep us from expressing ourselves creatively (Kelley & Kelley, 2013). For example, when a school staff is brainstorming new ways to approach the schoolwide writing assessments during a professional development session, it can feel daunting to take creative risks and offer novel ways to teach writing if we don't feel psychologically safe within the social environment. If we sense that people have the capacity for groupthink or that they will discount our ideas in a disrespectful way, it can be nearly impossible to be vulnerable by offering up our fresh, unproven ideas.

As we discussed in chapter 2 (page 43), reframing negative self-talk is an important step in avoiding self-sabotaging behaviors when it comes to taking creative risks. Whether we are planning a new cross-curricular unit on chicks or learning to paint with watercolors, accessing a more positive inner monologue makes the creative journey more pleasant, and therefore more sustainable. The same applies to our creative approaches within social settings. To increase creativity in our classrooms and schools, we need to promote psychologically safe environments. So much of that psychological safety comes from the words we use. Words crystalize and embody values. As Kelley and Kelley (2013) state, "language is the crystallization of thought . . . to change attitudes and behaviors, it helps to first change the vernacular" (p. 198).

When it comes to our collective creative endeavors like group planning for school goals at the beginning of the year, working in our collaborative teams on shared planning and learning goals, and setting the tone for classwide collaboration, there are some key phrases that can curtail creativity before it even has a chance to flourish, while other sayings can fuel the collective creative fire. Table 5.1 (page 144) reflects examples of creativity extinguishers and fuelers (adapted from Kelley & Kelley, 2013).

TABLE 5.1: PHRASES THAT EXTINGUISH AND FUEL CREATIVITY

Phrases That Extinguish Creativity	Phrases That Fuel Creativity
• We always do it this way!	• That's a new idea. Tell me more!
• That won't work!	• What might this new idea help us do?
• We've already tried that, and it failed.	• Why? Why? Why?
• That's a bad idea.	• I could if . . .
• I can't do that.	• What can I add to make it even better?
• There's no way they will be able to do it!	• How might we . . . ?
• Nobody does it that way.	• Wouldn't it be cool if . . . ?
• No.	• Yes!
• I don't like that idea at all!	• I like . . . (positive feedback)
	• I wish . . . (constructive feedback)

Source: Adapted from Kelley & Kelley, 2013.

The fear of judgement can be a real deterrent to sharing our creative ideas and approaches with others. At the end of the day, instead of *staying small* to avoid judgement, it is worthwhile to examine the message you wish to share with others and do so courageously. As Kelley and Kelley (2013) assert, "Normalcy is overrated. If you tap into your natural creativity, you have a chance to be extraordinary" (p. 246). Don't play small. Be courageous. Make your voice heard, despite the fear of judgement. Your ideas just might have a tremendous and innovative impact on the way your school or community operates.

Perceived Lack of Resources

It is possible to feel held back in our creativity because of a perceived lack of resources. It's easy to avoid creative expression because of the perception that you don't have the necessary resources to be successful, which can fuel procrastination or even avoiding a task altogether (Jarvis, 2019). We've discussed time as a resource, but money, too, can be a perceived roadblock to creativity.

Though it can be nice to work with high-quality, high-cost materials and tools in our professional and personal lives as educators, often our resourcefulness alone can fuel creativity. Constraints can paradoxically stretch our creative capabilities; they can actually "fuel creativity" (Comstock, 2018, p. 124). As educators, so many of us are accustomed to doing incredible work with students within the context of tight constraints: tight timelines and tight budgets. Kelley and Kelley

(2013) reinforce, "Instead of letting a lack of resources hold you back, use these constraints to be creative and come up with solutions that require minimal time and money" (p. 249). For instance, using a smartphone instead of a state-of-the-art camera to take photographs can result in beautiful, meaningful photographs. Moreover, I know educators who teach their art students to make pinhole cameras to capture photographs in class, using recycled materials. Cost should not be a barrier to expressing our creativity. Instead, we simply need to ask ourselves to think outside the box. Think, *What can I do within the context of this limited resource?*

There are many reasons that prevent us from exploring our own creativity and sense of play in our lives as educators. The truth is unspent creativity is a catalyst for restlessness and discontent. Everyone has the capacity for creativity. It is not a *talent*; it is a *practice*. We can lean into our passions and interests to feel more fulfilled and happier in our lives as educators.

Strategies to Ignite Your True Self Fire

Creativity in education is essential for preparing your students for the future, but it is also a fundamental component in your wellness as an individual. As you've learned, play, innovation, and creativity are not always readily accessible to you as an adult, for a myriad of reasons. In this section, you will explore how to foster a creative mindset and how to establish creative practices to lean into your creativity as an educator for the benefit of your students and for your own benefit, professionally and personally.

Strategies for Fostering a Creative Mindset

Your mindset in play and creativity is important. You may have preconceived ideas about your limitations and capabilities when it comes to tapping into your own creativity. These strategies will enable you to craft a creative, intentional mindset through a curiosity audit, learning to keep an open mind, challenging your inner perfectionist to adopt a done-is-better-than-perfect mindset, accepting that everything is a remix, and avoiding creative sabotage with a few simple phrases. Each of the strategies is followed by a tactical exercise that enables you to develop your creativity in a very real and practical way.

The Curiosity Audit

This exercise helps you to gain clarity about some of the common themes that elicit a sense of curiosity in your personal and professional life. In highlighting themes or curiosities, it can be fun to explore them further, in a more deliberate way (see "Template for the Curiosity Audit," page 158).

- **Common themes:** Examine your music, books, magazines, photographs, wall hangings, travel experiences, décor, and physical environment. What are some common themes that tend to come up again and again?

  For example, perhaps you see an overarching ocean theme within the music you listen to, the books you read, the photographs on your wall, and the places you travel. How can you bring your love of the ocean to the forefront, in your teaching and in your personal life?

- **Expansive or constrictive:** When it comes to deciding whether to pursue a curiosity, author and podcaster Marie Forleo (2019), explains the importance of tuning into whether something feels *expansive* or *constricting* (Forleo, 2019). Many of our decisions are intuitive. Constrictive ideas tend to leave us feeling uptight, worried, and creatively uninspired; we generally shouldn't pursue them. When we feel expansive, we feel open to new possibilities, optimistic, and more creative—these are intuitive markers that can encourage us to explore new curiosities. When you think of your creative endeavor, do you feel expansive or constricted?

  For example, while I may love teaching students to write within the classroom, the prospect of going on a three-day grammar retreat leaves me feeling constricted. I may continue to pursue my passion for fostering my students' love of writing through other avenues instead, such as attending inspiring webinars hosted by some of my favorite children's authors (a more expansive, inspired experience). It's possible that your deep dive will enable you to co-create a powerful historical fiction unit for your English classes, or you might even want to explore writing your own historical fiction short story.

- **Walk the talk:** Our interests and curiosity tend to bubble over into our personal and professional lives. What do you tend to talk about with friends, family, students, and parents? Are you knowledgeable about particular topics?

  For instance, every lunch recess, you sit down with colleagues and discuss your current book pick of the week. Generally, you choose historical fiction, and so does your friend. Realizing your shared passion for this genre, you both commit to reading and discussing twenty of the top-reviewed historical fiction novels throughout the next year.

The "Yes, and . . ." Improvisation Game

When brainstorming, especially in teams, staff meetings, and classrooms, it can be difficult for people to accept all answers without judgement in the beginning phase. Interestingly, some of the most ridiculous ideas can spur and inspire realistic or innovative solutions. Often, fear plays a role in muzzling those with wacky ideas—people are often afraid of being judged or ridiculed. This partner-based activity allows creativity to flow freely (along with some laughs).

The purpose of "Yes, and . . ." is to encourage nonjudgement and divergent thinking in a team setting. This is an especially helpful exercise if a team is about to do some big-picture brainstorming for the school, for example. You could use the seven-step exercise as a warm-up for a professional development day or a team-building day.

1. Find a partner.

2. The first partner suggests an activity, starting the phrase with "Let's . . ." (For example, "Let's paint a boat.")

3. The second person responds by saying, "Yes, and . . ." and adds to the first partner's suggestion. (For example, "Yes, and let's use blue paint.")

4. Every ensuing phrase starts with "Yes, and . . ."

5. End the game after five to ten turns.

6. Switch partners and repeat the exercise.

7. Share realizations, commentary, and challenges about the activity using the following questions: *What did you learn? What was easy? What was challenging for you?*

The Done Is Better Than Perfect Challenge

One of the most helpful mantras I have learned when it comes to tapping into my own creativity is the motto Sheryl Sandberg put on the walls at Facebook as a leader: *Done is better than perfect* (Groth, 2013). While at first glance this mantra may appear to encourage mediocre work, I assure you it does not.

When I first started my podcast, I created an introduction to the show that summed up the premise in a catchy twenty-second clip. When I started writing it, I felt paralyzed by the grandeur of having to craft such a seemingly important description. If I had cultivated a mindset that perseverated on how important or serious this task felt, I'm almost certain I would have never written the introduction, and I may never have actually completed my first interview for the show. Instead, I sat down in my seat once my children had gone to bed, and I started writing, keeping in mind my audience and the purpose of the podcast. The first three drafts were messy, imperfect, and not particularly eloquent. I revised the introduction, then shared with some trusted friends, then revised some more. Finally, it was as complete as it would ever need to be. I recorded and published the trailer.

Perfect is an impossibility. Whether you are writing report card comments, crafting a parent newsletter, painting, or taking a photograph, if you don't start somewhere, you'll never complete your work. If you get so hung up on everything needing to be perfect, you will literally prevent yourself from completing the art or the task. Sometimes, you simply need to tell yourself, "Done is better than perfect." While the following creative practice may not in itself be fruitful financially or socially, the practice of creating, committing to self-expression, and sharing your work with others is such an essential aspect of diving into your creativity. The more you do it, the better you'll get!

- Choose five quotes you love related to education, art, psychology, or any area of curiosity.

- Create a graphic for each of the quotes using a text-and-image program like Canva (www.canva.com). Make sure you properly attribute credit to the author. Do not spend longer than five minutes on the graphics. Remind yourself, *Done is better than perfect!*

- Every day for five days, post one of the five graphic quotes and riff about the theme. Give yourself a tight timeline (five to fifteen minutes maximum) so you don't allow yourself to dive too deeply into perfecting mode. Remind yourself, *Done is better than perfect!*

You can use the following prompts to help you come up with meaningful commentary.

- Is there a meaningful personal story that comes to mind to illustrate the quote?

- Is there a dominant emotion that is evoked from the quote? What is it, and how does it apply to the current sociopolitical environment?

- Who does the quote remind you of? Is there a story you might be able to share?

- How has the quote helped you or someone you know to reach their higher potential, gain clarity, or be more peaceful?

Once you've checked your commentary for basic spelling, conventions, and typos, and you're happy-ish with the post (remember, you'll never be 100 percent satisfied), post to a social media account. If you're feeling self-conscious about being attributed to this work because it feels foreign, create a pseudonym account on social media and post to that account. Remember, *Done is better than perfect.*

Reflect after five days on how it felt to create and share your work. Don't get caught up in the likes on social media. The extrinsic recognition you receive or don't receive is not a measure of your worth. This activity is about getting comfortable with the discomfort of embracing your own creativity.

The Everyday Photo Five-Day Challenge

Many of us in education are full-fledged perfectionists or *recovering* perfectionists, meaning that we take great pride in our work, the small details, and hold ourselves (and others) to an exceedingly high set of expectations (Mahmoodi-Shahrebabaki, 2016). Whether we are writing report cards, thinking up a new winter holiday parent gift, planning a new social justice inquiry unit about Indigenous rights, or planning for parent-teacher interviews, it's challenging not to be hard on ourselves when our abilities or tasks fall short of our vision. How many times have you planned a lesson, only to have it flop when you tried it in front of a class? It's common. Like many artists, educators have high expectations of themselves and their outcomes.

As we try new things, we must cling to the knowledge that we will get better at what we do, but we have to be patient with ourselves during our first attempts. No *overnight success* ever happened *overnight*. It is usually a slow-drip approach. Just keep your mind alighted with what matters. Whenever I teach my primary students art, I always say, "There are no mistakes in art!" Every attempt in creativity adds value through experience.

As Anne Lamott (1995) states in her book *Bird by Bird*,

> All good writers write [terrible first drafts] . . . very few writers really know what they are doing until they've done it. Nor do they go about their business feeling dewy and thrilled. They do not type a few stiff warm-up sentences and then find themselves bounding along like huskies across the snow. (p. 21)

We must be willing to fail gloriously, accept our terrible first attempts at creativity, and understand that for some time, our taste (and expectations) will supersede our abilities at the beginning.

The purpose of the everyday photo five-day challenge is to use your eyes to find and experience the art in the everyday moments (Younger, 2019). Creativity enables you to see the world through a more sensory-oriented lens, and this activity is designed to get you out of your *head* and into your *senses*. Another essential aspect to this activity is suspending your self-judgement and simply accepting your attempts at creativity (including your terrible first draft). Place your smartphone or camera by your bed the night before completing this activity and use the "Template for the Everyday Photo Five-Day Challenge" (page 160) as a guide.

The Thirty Circles Exercise

Originality is impractical. For most creative exploits related to education, it's more helpful to think of our tasks as being authentic. Most of the ideas we get are a result of cross-pollination between ideas that already exist and our own perspective. In other words, most of the ideas we come across are a remix of established concepts with a twist. In education, this kind of cross-pollination is a blessing because it offers fresh methods to teaching while maintaining our own integrity.

Adapted from Kelley and Kelley's (2013) book *Creative Confidence*, the thirty circles exercise invites you to take thirty blank circles on a sheet of regular-sized paper and use your divergent thinking to turn them into familiar objects within the time frame of three minutes. It exercises your creativity by helping you think outside the box (or circle, in this case). This three-step exercise can be completed independently, in partners, or even in a large group. You can conduct it with students and adults alike. It lends itself well to professional development team building and creativity warm-ups.

1. Give each person a sheet of paper with thirty circles predrawn or copied onto it.

2. Instruct participants to use a pen or pencil and turn the circles into as many everyday objects as they can within a three-minute window. For example, a basketball, a fish tank, a baseball, a bulls-eye target, a clock, and so on.

3. When the three minutes are up, take stock of the results. How many circles did people manage to fill in? How detailed are the drawings? How many are literal representations of objects (balls) and how many are divergent, creative interpretations of the circle (hats, planets, cookies)? How many people went outside the confines of the rules by connecting the circles or making the circles unrecognizable?

Repurposing and reimagining everyday objects (in this case, circles) allows you to practice seeing differently and expands your capacity for divergent thinking. Additionally, this exercise is a great way to increase fluency of fresh new ideas. It would be a wonderful way to start a professional development problem-solving session.

Strategies to Establish a Strong Creative Practice

A strong creative mindset alone will not enable you to lean into your creativity. Routines and practices reinforce your vision and desire to be creative. You need to be consistent in your approach to creativity as it is a process that requires discipline and consistency (Jarvis, 2019). In this section, you will explore common approaches that invite the practice of creativity into your life, including allowing your mind to be idle, giving yourself time to rest, exploring novel experiences as a means of diversifying your perspective, seeking out opportunities for play, dedicating yourself to a creative schedule, and surrounding yourself with supportive and encouraging individuals who value the risks you are taking and share your journey alongside you.

Let Your Mind Be Idle Activity

Mind-wandering—which is similar to daydreaming, where your mind wanders from topic to topic without much structure or deliberate focus—boosts divergent thinking, allowing our minds to explore a myriad of different approaches and avenues before settling on one (Grant, 2016). Have you ever driven from your house to the grocery store, only to arrive and realize it's almost as though your mind was transported elsewhere for the journey, prompted by the environmental stimuli and circumstances occurring in your life? If so, you've experienced mind-wandering. When we are too focused on a goal, the result is that we can shut down our capacity for divergent thinking (Grant, 2016). Choosing to engage in low-concentration activities is the key to entering an idle state of mind (Grant, 2016). If we are working on a particular problem, it might even be helpful to pose the problem as a question. For example, if you are struggling with student engagement during mathematics class, you could ask yourself, "How can I engage my learners more effectively during math class through hands-on means?" Giving yourself a subconscious focal point can result in some interesting solutions when your mind is wandering.

The following are some easy ways to let your mind wander.

- Take a shower.
- Go for a walk.

- Unload the dishwasher.

- Stretch.

- Paint your nails.

- Clean a room.

- Engage in repetitive actions (for example, knitting, needlepoint, coloring, gardening).

- Do easy data entry.

- Address envelopes.

- File paperwork.

- Pack lunches.

- Fold laundry.

- Mow the lawn.

Novel Experiences Challenge

To boost your own professional and personal creativity, this two-step challenge invites you to step outside of the status quo and your comfortable routine to embrace the exciting discomfort and learning that come from novel experiences.

1. On your own or with a colleague, choose an activity or experience that you've never done before. Commit to take on this new experience within the next month (with classes, one may need to allow for additional time for booking and scheduling).

    The following is a list of novel experience ideas that you might like to attempt.

    - Take a pottery class.

    - Try a new recipe.

    - Take a watercolor class.

    - Create a website.

    - Take a continuing studies class unrelated to education at your local college.

    - Listen to speaker discuss a topic that is new to you.

    - Take a cooking class.

    - Go to a book launch at your local bookstore.

- Take a cake decorating class.

- Join a book club.

- Start a new exercise program (for example, Zumba class, weight lifting, yoga).

- Volunteer at a soup kitchen.

- Take a new route to work.

- Switch classes with another teacher for a day.

- Think of some topics and record your reflections on voice memos and listen back.

- Interview someone you respect about something he or she is good at (even the act of formulating questions is creative).

- Spice up your regular Saturday night spaghetti sauce by changing a few ingredients.

- Write a song.

- Learn a new sport.

- Write a poem.

- Write in your journal.

- Take up sketch-noting, a creative style of visual note-taking that relies heavily on hand-drawn graphic text, icons, and simple images.

- Learn to make origami.

- Learn to make friendship bracelets.

- Put out a YouTube Explainer video.

- Learn a new video game.

- Learn how to use a new app.

- Go to a museum.

- Go see a movie in a genre you'd never normally opt to watch (take note of new learnings or observations you make about the genre).

- Go see a music performance.

- Talk to a colleague whom you've never really talked to at length.

- Draw some arbitrary circles on a page and seek out recognizable shapes within them.

- Learn a new approach to mathematics or literacy.

- Take a professional development workshop geared at a different age group than the one you teach.

- Challenge yourself to create a daily doodle for the next month.

2. After you've had the experience (whether it is a six-week pottery course or a one-time death-metal concert performance), ask yourself some of the following questions in order to open yourself to the benefits of cross-pollination. Record the answers using a journal or your phone.

- How might this experience help me think about my work in education in a new way?

- How might I apply the processes and approaches from this experience to my classroom?

- How does this experience enable me to think about my students, school, and colleagues differently?

- What's not working, professionally or personally, that this experience could help me fix?

- What are some things that made me feel uncomfortable during this experience? How might I relate this to my students' experience of learning new things? How might I make their experience more engaging, fun, or interesting?

- What did I learn that challenged some of my existing assumptions about this craft, experience, or community that I might be able to apply to education or my own life?

- In what ways might I incorporate this challenge into my life as a regular reminder to disrupt the status quo?

The Rate My Day Activity

Recreation and play allow you to invite creativity and divergent thinking into your life because you are not actively operating from a linear mode (Seppälä, 2017). Play also alters your mood in a positive way. Barbara Fredrickson (2013), a professor and psychology researcher at the University of North Carolina, finds that when you experience positive emotions, you are better able to focus on a task and see the big picture. Seeing the big picture allows you to make innovative creative connections that linear thinking might miss (Fredrickson, 2013). Alternatively, when you deny yourself the opportunity for play, you can see detrimental effects to your well-being and relationship health. As Stuart Brown, head of the National Institute for Play, states, "What you begin to see when there's major play deprivation in an otherwise competent adult is that they're not much fun to be around. . . . You begin to see that the perseverance and joy in work is lessened and that life is much more laborious" (as cited in Yenigun, 2014). You need to be childlike in your approach to life, asking yourself, "What fills me with childlike joy, awe, and happiness?" and then *doing* more of that (Fredrickson, 2013).

The five-step rate my day activity is designed to help you gain perspective about your everyday patterns and habits related to play and fun, an important aspect of stoking the fire of creativity (Kelley & Kelley, 2013).

1. Every night for one to two weeks, before heading to bed, take time to reflect on your day.

2. In a journal or on your phone, record your reflections and take a moment to rate your day in terms of the fun you had. On a scale of 0–10, how much fun did you have during the day?

3. Each day, take note of the activities that contribute to your overall sense of having fun versus the activities that do not seem fun to you.

4. At the end of the one- to two-week observation, notice the patterns of activity that contribute to your sense of happiness, playfulness, and joy.

5. Make a commitment to actively incorporate more joyful and playful activities into your day, especially if you're feeling overwhelmed.

Finding an Ideal Creative Support Network Exercise

When it comes to feeling comfortable in expressing yourself, belonging and psychological safety is paramount (B. Brown, 2013). To remain committed to your own creative endeavors, it's important to surround yourself with people who support your newfound quest to express yourself fully, who explore the world with a sense of curiosity and awe, and who respect your desire to write a new story for yourself. These days, in our highly connected, globalized world, it's never been easier to find like-minded people (Petriglieri, 2018). Sometimes, they will be people you work with or friends. Often, however, the people you work with, your family, or those with whom you are connected socially will not fit the bill as a creative support network (Burgess, 2012). Choose people who choose *you*. Don't feel like you need to bend yourself into a pretzel trying to explain to people who don't understand why you're taking a new class, approaching curriculum in a new way, or now unavailable on Tuesday nights.

Sometimes, family and friends may not be as invested in your journey as you are or may not understand the creative risks you're taking (Burgess, 2012). Instead, you may have to seek out creatively supportive people elsewhere. Seeking account-ability, belonging, and camaraderie as you experiment with self-expression is a wonderful way to expand your social network. While finding people who support and love you unconditionally is important, your creative support network should consist of people who care about the work you're doing, are engaged in your jour-ney, and are invested in your creativity, meaning they have some skin in the game themselves. According to Petriglieri (2018), the following are a few key elements to look for in a support network.

- A supportive yet strong group culture to fuel you with courage and comfort

- A group in which learning is prioritized over performance

- A group that allows for give and take, as a range of abilities enables the free flow of expertise and questioning

There are many fun, easy, and productive ways to form a creative supportive network (see figure 5.1 for examples).

Conclusion

Many folks, especially in education, undermine and discount their own capacity for creativity. The truth is that we are all capable of expressing ourselves creatively; however, roadblocks related to perfectionism, unrealistic expectations, and fear of failure hold many of us back from experiencing the true magic of accessing our own creativity. When we cultivate our creative muscle, we gain the ability to access our creative, divergent thinking more readily, which helps us to solve problems, interact with the world more wholeheartedly, and feel happier overall.

Nothing can protect us from creative failure. In fact, the iterative process is what teaches us creative resiliency and allows us to explore new ways of experi-encing the world around us. Many of us lose our ability for creative expression as adults because we become fearful of failure or ridicule. Like a muscle, we can train ourselves to regain our creative self-expression to live a more wholehearted, expressive life.

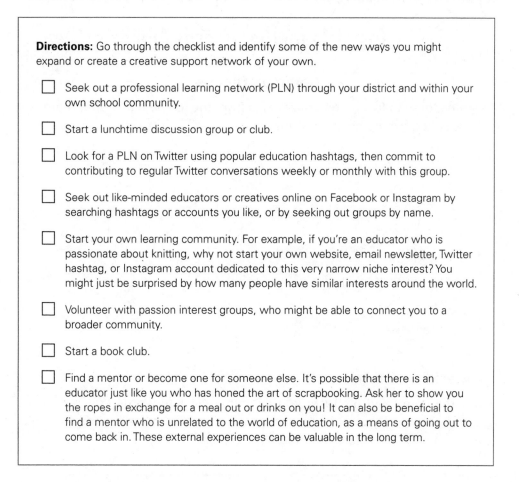

Directions: Go through the checklist and identify some of the new ways you might expand or create a creative support network of your own.

☐ Seek out a professional learning network (PLN) through your district and within your own school community.

☐ Start a lunchtime discussion group or club.

☐ Look for a PLN on Twitter using popular education hashtags, then commit to contributing to regular Twitter conversations weekly or monthly with this group.

☐ Seek out like-minded educators or creatives online on Facebook or Instagram by searching hashtags or accounts you like, or by seeking out groups by name.

☐ Start your own learning community. For example, if you're an educator who is passionate about knitting, why not start your own website, email newsletter, Twitter hashtag, or Instagram account dedicated to this very narrow niche interest? You might just be surprised by how many people have similar interests around the world.

☐ Volunteer with passion interest groups, who might be able to connect you to a broader community.

☐ Start a book club.

☐ Find a mentor or become one for someone else. It's possible that there is an educator just like you who has honed the art of scrapbooking. Ask her to show you the ropes in exchange for a meal out or drinks on you! It can also be beneficial to find a mentor who is unrelated to the world of education, as a means of going out to come back in. These external experiences can be valuable in the long term.

Figure 5.1: Ideas for finding an ideal creative support network.

In this chapter, we've discovered specific approaches related to *flow*; the research on the value of creativity in schools (specifically for teachers); information on perfectionism, procrastination, and creative roadblocks; and the importance of sharing our creative work with others. My hope is that you courageously step into your creative potential and allow yourself the capacity to discover the world around you in a new, more expansive way.

Template for the Curiosity Audit

Common Themes

Examine three to five items or activities from the following list that represent well-rounded examples of your interests.

- Magazines
- Books
- Music genres
- Clothing style
- Décor inspiration
- Travel experiences
- Hobbies
- Significant events
- Art
- Entertainment or movies

From the items and interests you examine, list five words that reflect the general themes that come up for you within the interests (for example, *surfing, outdoors, beach, volunteering, rustic*).

_____

Expansive or Constrictive

How does pursuing each of the five themes further within your own life feel for you, professionally and personally? List the five words again and indicate whether you feel a sense of expansiveness or constriction, on a scale of 1–5, when you think of diving deeper into this interest.

_____ Constrictive 1   2   3   4   5   Expansive

_____ Constrictive 1   2   3   4   5   Expansive

_____ Constrictive 1   2   3   4   5   Expansive

_____ Constrictive 1   2   3   4   5   Expansive

_____ Constrictive 1   2   3   4   5   Expansive

Page 1 of 2

Walk the Talk

Take a moment to reflect on the following questions.

- What are the top two passions that seem most expansive to you?

- Are you surprised by those passions?

- What are you currently doing in your life that reflects these passions?

- Are these topics that come up for you often in conversation at school and in your personal life?

- How are these two topics related or different?

- What might you be able to do to further your interests?

_____

_____

_____

_____

Template for the Everyday Photo Five-Day Challenge

Day	Task Description	Reflection
One	1. Wake up and immediately use your smartphone or camera to take a picture of something you notice as significant or vivid as you are lying in your bed. 2. Take another photo while you are sitting up in bed. 3. Take another photo from your bathroom, at breakfast, and as you head out the door. 4. Take at least four to five photos in the morning before you leave your house.	What did you capture? What do you notice? What do you wonder? What did you see for the first time, in a different way?
Two	1. Repeat the activity, but do it at the end of the day. 2. Take a photo during your bedtime preparation routine. 3. Take a photo while you are sitting in your bed. 4. Take a photo as you are lying in bed. 5. Capture at least four to five photos.	What did you capture? What do you notice? What do you wonder? What stands out about your nightly routine that is different from the morning?

Page 1 of 3

Day	Task Description	Reflection
Three	1. Take photos of your workday. 2. Take some macro shots (up-close pictures) of tools you use (your keyboard, pens, whiteboard, sticky notes, student work). 3. Take some zoom-outs of your experience (panoramic shots of your school campus, the lunchroom). 4. Select four to five photos that stand out for you about your day.	What did you capture? What do you notice? What do you wonder? What about the experience of capturing your workday changed the experience of work for you? What small details became new observations for you?
Four	1. Take photos when you tend to want to use your phone as a distraction (on the bus, as you prepare dinner, while your children are arguing, at night as you watch a show). 2. Choose only four to five stand-out shots.	What did you capture? What do you notice? What do you wonder? What stands out for you?

Page 2 of 3

Day	*Task Description*	*Reflection*
Five	1. Review or print the photos from the previous four days. You should have about twenty photos to work with, by this point. 2. Lay them all out on a table, wall, or bulletin board.	What do you see for the first time, in a different way? What does this tell you about your environment and lived experience? What stands out the most for you about this experience? How does this experience change the way you view the seemingly mundane moments in life? How might you use this activity within the classroom or with your school staff to promote the adoption of the terrible-first-attempts mindset?

REIGNITE

Craft Your Own Road Maps to Go From Burnt Out to Fired Up

Our job in this lifetime is not to shape ourselves into some ideal we imagine we ought to be, but to find out who we already are and become it.

—Wayne Dyer

The purposes of this book have been twofold: (1) explore research, real-life stories, scenarios, and actionable strategies connected to fired-up living and educating, and (2) unveil a road map for success and thriving as an educator. You've read the book and completed the activities, so now what? Well, now, my dear friends, it's time to tie it all together using *reignite road maps*.

The following five individual thematic road maps are designed to help you create lasting habits and meaningful practices to reignite your passion in the classroom, in the spirit of reflecting, reframing, refocusing, reconnecting, and revealing your creative self. Visit **go.SolutionTree.com/teacherefficacy** to download each road map as a reproducible PDF.

While any of these themes can be explored out of sequence, the progression through each of the five themes enables you to build on your previous insights, accomplishments, and goals from the book. You may explore each of the five themes individually through quiet reflection after school, on the weekend, or during regular school breaks like summer vacation or spring break. However, there is tremendous additional value in reflecting on mindfulness, self-compassion, goal setting, connection, and creativity alongside colleagues within the context of professional development seminars, school book club conversations, or education Twitter chats. However you decide to approach the reignite road maps, be sure to share your learning with others. To learn on your own is a wonderful gift to yourself, but to share your learning and insights with others can result in profound, immeasurable, and positive results.

This chapter contains the following road maps.

- My Reflect Road Map (page 165)
- My Reframe Road Map (page 168)
- My Refocus Road Map (page 172)
- My Reconnect Road Map (page 173)
- My Reveal Road Map (page 175)

My Reflect Road Map

When educators become so used to functioning through overwhelming feelings or when they numb uncomfortable emotions, it can be challenging to become attuned to their own struggles, both in and out of the classroom. The first step in reigniting your inner fire as an educator is engaging in honest self-reflection, self-compassion, and true self-care.

Take a moment to go through the checklist in figure 1.1 on page 13 to see if you are exhibiting any signs of burnout. If you find yourself ticking a lot of the boxes, it could signal a need to reconsider some of the habits, routines, and approaches in your life. Explore the following six questions and prompts as a means of reflecting on your inner needs, triggers, responses, and mindfulness practices.

1. If you were to rank your emotional needs (certainty, variety, significance, belonging, growth, contribution), what would be your top three needs, in order of importance?

   a. _____

   b. _____

   c. _____

2. What are some positive and negative ways you tend to meet your emotional needs, especially when you are under stress? For example, if certainty is important to you, perhaps you like to have an air-tight morning routine, or perhaps you tend to overprepare for every possible scenario when you are in uncertain times.

Emotional Need	Positive Ways I Meet My Emotional Needs	Negative Ways I Meet My Emotional Needs
1.		
2.		
3.		

Page 1 of 3

From Burnt Out to Fired Up © 2022 Solution Tree Press • SolutionTree.com
Visit **go.SolutionTree.com/teacherefficacy** to download this free reproducible.

3. Think of a time you felt stressed or overwhelmed. Describe the situation in a few sentences.

How did you respond to the stress with yourself, with others, and through your actions? When you are stressed or triggered, is your tendency to go into fight, flight, or freeze mode? For example, do you tend to get defensive (fight), escape to your favorite book or show (flight), or have a difficult time with decision making (freeze)? Write down some of your initial responses to these questions.

4. Reflect on a few of the triggers that most commonly contribute to your stress and overwhelm. When we can recognize and name our triggering patterns, it becomes easier to predict and counteract their effects.

   a. What tends to bother you most when you are stressed? For example, the sound of my children's whining can be particularly trying when I am overwhelmed by school stressors.

   b. What are some ways you might be able to anticipate or counteract some of those stressors so they become less surprising for you or more manageable?

Triggers	*Anticipatory Action*

5. When you feel triggered emotionally, what are three things that tend to make you feel better?

6. Reflection is a practice. Choose and record one of the strategies from chapter 1 (page 26)—mindful awareness, self-compassion, or common humanity—in the following log. Use the log to record and document your progress throughout the week as you commit to practicing every day. Check off each day that you complete the strategy. At the end of the week, reflect on the following questions. Continue with the strategy for the rest of the month and reflect again, or choose a new strategy for the following week and repeat the process.

Self-Compassion Focus Strategy:						
Sunday	Monday	Tuesday	Wednesday	Thursday	Friday	Saturday

Journal Prompts:

1. How did the strategy decrease my overall feeling of overwhelm?

2. What worked best for me? What didn't work?

3. How might I incorporate this strategy into my daily practice as a way to promote reflection and self-compassion?

My Reframe Road Map

Carve out some quiet space to reflect on the following questions related to reframing and resilience. If you have an opportunity, through professional development or a book club discussion, explore these questions through conversation. If it feels comfortable, have each of the group members share their reflections in partners, in small groups, or even within the whole group, to build a sense of common humanity with your colleagues or collaborative team. While these reflections can bring up personal struggles that may not be appropriate to share within a large group, many of the coping strategies and resilience tools may be powerful to share in a round-table discussion.

1. Think about a time when you had to overcome a difficult situation in your life. How did you overcome the challenge?

2. What are some learnings you gained as a result? How have you applied that learning to other challenging circumstances in your life since then?

3. What are some ways that people helped you? How might you be able to offer support to someone going through a similar struggle?

Page 1 of 4

4. How do you tend to respond to shame? Circle your preferred "shame shield" on the following table that seems to protect you from the pain of shameful experiences. List some of the common ways you tend to respond when you are ashamed of something.

Moving Toward *(Pleasing)*	*Moving Away* *(Escaping)*	*Moving Against* *(Fighting)*

5. Fill in the following table by reflecting on the following questions:

   a. How has your shame shield served you positively?

   b. How has this shield hurt you or others, affecting you negatively?

   c. Does the shield still serve you?

How has my shame shield *served me positively?*	*How has my shame shield* *affected my life negatively?*

6. We all hold limiting beliefs about ourselves. What are three of the most challenging thoughts and beliefs you would like to overcome? How might overcoming these negative perceptions help you reframe challenges and become more resilient? How might overcoming these beliefs help you achieve some of the dreams you have for yourself?

Page 2 of 4

My dominant limiting beliefs	*How might letting go of this belief benefit me or those I love?*

7. Have you ever encountered toxic positivity? What are some examples of toxic positivity that have served as more of a hindrance to resilience than a help?

8. Self-regulation allows us to gain more control over our immediate situations by decreasing unhelpful stressors to build our potential for resiliency. Of the five stress domains (physical, emotional, cognitive, social, and prosocial), name one area you would like to focus on and set a goal to decrease just one stressor in that area this week. For example, perhaps the messiness of your workspace is getting overwhelming. Therefore, you might set a goal to decrease the physical stressor of the messy desk by spending your prep time cleaning it up.

Target Stress Domain (Circle one)	1. Physical 2. Emotional 3. Cognitive 4. Social 5. Prosocial
Action Goal	This week, I will work to reduce my _____ stress by _____. I know I will have achieved my goal when _____ _____.
Reflect: How did targeting this stress domain decrease my overall sense of overwhelm? Would I continue this habit? Why or why not?	

My Refocus Road Map

Goal setting is an important aspect of refocusing our attention on what truly matters to us as educators. It is essential to regularly set aside time to take stock of our inner desires and grandiose goals, write them down, discuss them with our loved ones and colleagues, and give them air to breathe. Throughout chapter 3 (page 65), there are a number of detailed, action-oriented activities for goal setting. For the purposes of this road map, I'd like you to think more broadly about your goals to anchor your vision of the path you'd like to take and your arrival destination.

Take some time to reflect on the following four questions. Record your response in a journal or discuss with a friend or colleague to deepen your thinking.

1. In your career and personal life, what are some of your most important goals?

2. How will you get to where you want to go? Generally, what are some of the big-picture action steps you need to take to arrive at your desired goal destination?

3. How will you know you have arrived? What are some of the markers that will indicate success to you?

4. How will achieving your goals and tapping into your purpose contribute to your feeling of being reignited?

My Reconnect Road Map

When it comes to building positive social relationships in our personal and professional lives as teachers, trust, vulnerability, perspective-taking, and recognition are important aspects that contribute to our well-being. Think about the relationships you have in your professional life as a teacher and within your personal life. How do you show up for others? How does your interactive style affect your communication and relationships? Reflect on a few or all of the following seven questions to gain a deeper understanding of your ability to connect, develop relationships, and demonstrate social awareness.

1. Who matters most to you in your professional and personal circle? Name two to five people maximum.

2. How can you nurture the relationships that matter to you most?

3. How do you show gratitude to those who are important to you?

4. How does your communication approach with people impact your personal and professional relationships? How do people generally feel after an interaction with you? How do you want them to feel after they have interacted with you? Do people tend to trust you? How do you know?

5. What are some of your favorite ways to build rapport with students, parents, administrators, and colleagues?

Page 1 of 2

6. When it comes to your connections with colleagues, students, parents, administrators, friends, and family, what are you most proud of?

7. This week, commit to learning the names of two to three people you don't know well (students in your school, the new teacher down the hall who took over for your colleague's maternity leave, the barista at your local coffee shop, the substitute teacher whose name you've never learned) by using one or more of the methods listed in figure 4.1 (page 123).

Circumstance Description	Name Strategy	Reflection
Example: I decided to learn the name of our stand-in janitor, who is filling in for our current custodian's leave. She comes into my class every day, but I haven't really had a chance to learn her name.	Spell it!	I asked the replacement custodian what her name was today and learned that it was Caitlyn. I asked her to spell it for me, since her name has so many variations. All week, I've called her by name, and it's allowed us to open the door to some deeper conversations in the morning. I'm really getting to know her!

My Reveal Road Map

Creativity is accessible to all human beings, even though many adults experience a sense of disconnection from their own ability to be creative. Reflecting on our practices of creativity and drawing our attention to our day-to-day opportunities for creativity is an important final step that contributes to our ability to get fired up after feeling burnt out as educators. Creativity is an expression of ourselves and our spirit; it allows us to be fully human. In solitude, with some friends or colleagues, or through the more structured framework of a book club or a professional development discussion, explore the following four provocations and question sets as a means of digging deeper into your own creativity.

1. Take some time to compare and contrast your joyful creativity as a child and as an adult. Record your responses in the following table.

   a. As a child, what types of activities would tend to fill your soul?

   b. What creative activities bring you joy now?

Joyful Creativity in Childhood	*Joyful Creativity in Adulthood*
For example, making clothes for my dolls.	*For example, putting together color-coordinated outfits for teaching and posting them to Pinterest.*

What do you notice is similar about your joyful creativity as a child compared to your adult approach? What do you notice is different when it comes to your creative expression as a child versus as an adult?

Page 1 of 3

2. What are some of the creative roadblocks (see page 139) that hold you back from expressing yourself creatively? In the following figure, circle the ones th at tend to apply to you. How, specifically, do these roadblocks manifest themselves in your life?

Creativity Roadblock	Result
Time Confetti	
Procrastination	
Comparison	
Psychologically Unsafe Environment	
Playing Small	
Perceived Lack of Resources	

How might you counteract the roadblocks you experience through the activities highlighted in chapter 5 (page 145)? Choose one of the activities and describe how this might help you to counteract the roadblocks and open the door to creativity in your life. How might you apply this approach to your own practice as an educator, for the benefit of your students?

3. How might you establish a new creative practice or reestablish an existing one that means something to you? What action step could you take today toward that goal? Record your response in the following chart.

Creative Practice	*Action Step*
I'd like to start playing with watercolor paints again.	This weekend, I am going to purchase all the supplies I need for watercolor.

4. Set a creative goal for yourself this week, this month, and this year. How do you see yourself being creative in the short term, medium term, and long term?

Time Frame	*Creative Goal*
Short Term	This week, I will . . .
Medium Term	This month, I will . . .
Long Term	This year, I will . . .

Page 3 of 3

Closing Thoughts

It is my sincerest desire that you revisit your personal goals, desires, values, and dreams for your future as an educator. When you choose to author your own destiny, you have the power to live out a truly wholehearted and passionate existence. To be able to share that gift with your students, colleagues, friends, and loved ones is one of the most profound experiences any teacher can experience. You can regain and even deepen your passion. You can go from feeling burnt out to feeling fired up again! Together, through your intentional acts, you can effect immeasurable positive change.

References and Resources

Achor, S. (2010). *The happiness advantage: The seven principles of positive psychology that fuel success and performance at work.* New York: Crown Business.

Ackerman, C. (2021). *28 benefits of gratitude and most significant research findings.* Accessed at https://positivepsychology.com/benefits-gratitude-research-questions/ on July 16, 2021.

Aguilar, E. (2018). *Onward: Cultivating emotional resilience in educators.* San Francisco, CA: Jossey-Bass.

Alimujiang, A., Wiensch, A., Boss, J., Fleischer, N. L., Mondul, A. M., McLean, K., et al. (2019). Association between life purpose and mortality among US adults older than 50 years. *JAMA Network Open, 2*(5). Accessed at https://jamanetwork.com/journals/jamanetworkopen/fullarticle/2734064 on April 20, 2021.

Allen, J. (1951). *As a man thinketh.* Mount Vernon, NY: Peter Pauper Press.

Amabile, T. M., & Kramer, S. J. (2011). *The power of small wins.* Accessed at https://hbr.org/2011/05/the-power-of-small-wins on April 20, 2021.

Ambrose, S. A., Bridges, M. W., DiPietro, M., Lovett, M. C., & Norman, M. K. (2010). *How learning works: Seven research-based principles for smart teaching.* San Francisco, CA: Jossey-Bass.

American Federation of Teachers. (2017). *2017 educator quality of life survey.* Accessed at www.aft.org/2017-educator-quality-life-survey on July 20, 2021.

American Psychological Association. (2012). *Building your resilience.* Accessed at www.apa.org/helpcenter/road-resilience on June 8, 2021.

Anderman, E. M., & Anderman, L. H. (2014). *Classroom motivation* (2nd ed.). Boston: Pearson.

Anggina Neftyanic, C. C., Hariri, H., & Karwan, D. H. (2020). Do the transformation leadership style have a massive influence on teacher job satisfaction? *International Journal of Current Science Research and Review, 3*(11), 125–130.

Anxiety and Depression Association of America. (n.d.a). *Facts & statistics.* Accessed at https://adaa.org/about-adaa/press-room/facts-statistics on October 1, 2020.

Anxiety and Depression Association of America. (n.d.b). *Understanding disorders: What is anxiety and depression?* Accessed at https://adaa.org/understanding-anxiety on June 5, 2020.

Baker, W. (2014). *5 ways to get better at asking for help.* Accessed at hbr.org/2014/12/5-ways-to-get-better-at-asking-for-help on April 20, 2021.

Barsade, S. G., & Gibson, D. E. (2007). Why does affect matter in organizations? *Academy of Management Perspectives, 21*(1), 36–59.

Bayles, D., & Orland, T. (1993). *Art and fear: Observations on the perils (and rewards) of artmaking.* Santa Barbara, CA: Capra.

Bell, R. (2020). *Everything is spiritual: Who we are and what we're doing here.* New York: St. Martin's.

Benson, K. (2017, October 4). The magic relationship ratio, according to science [Blog post]. *The Gottman Institute.* Accessed at www.gottman.com/blog/the-magic-relationship-ratio-according-science on June 5, 2020.

Berkman, E. T. (2018). The neuroscience of goals and behavior change. *Consulting Psychology Journal: Practice and Research, 70*(1), 28–44.

Berns-Zare, I. (2019, June 4). The importance of having a sense of purpose [Blog post]. *Psychology Today.* Accessed at www.psychologytoday.com/us/blog/flourish-and-thrive/201906/the-importance-having-sense-purpose on October 1, 2020.

Bilanow, T. (2011). Bouncing back from hard times [Blog post]. *The New York Times.* Accessed at https://well.blogs.nytimes.com/2011/01/03/bouncing-back-from-hard-times on October 12, 2020.

Bill and Melinda Gates Foundation. (2014). *Bill Gates Teaching and Learning Conference 2014.* Accessed at www.gatesfoundation.org/ideas/speeches/2014/03/bill-gates-teaching-and-learning-conference on July 20, 2021.

Borba, M. (2017). *UnSelfie: Why empathetic kids succeed in our all-about-me world.* New York: Touchstone.

Bouskila-Yam, O., & Kluger, A. N. (2011). Strength-based performance appraisal and goal setting. *Human Resource Management Review, 21*(2), 137–147.

Brackett, M. (2019). *Permission to feel: Unlocking the power of emotions to help our kids, ourselves, and our society thrive.* New York: Celadon Books.

Bratman, G. N., Daily, G. C., Levy, B. J., & Gross, J. J. (2015). The benefits of nature experience: Improved affect and cognition. *Landscape and Urban Planning, 138,* 41–50.

Breton, T. (2018). *Professor Jennifer Fugate consults with Malcolm Gladwell on his latest book.* Accessed at www.umassd.edu/feature-stories/2018/jen-fugate.html on April 28, 2021.

Breuning, L. G. (2016). *Habits of a happy brain: Retrain your brain to boost your serotonin, dopamine, oxytocin, and endorphin levels.* Avon, MA: Adams Media.

Brodrick, M. (2019, April 18). The heart and science of kindness [Blog post]. *Harvard Health Blog.* Accessed at www.health.harvard.edu/blog/the-heart-and -science-of-kindness-2019041816447 on November 22, 2020.

Brooks, K. (2013, April 29). Stuck, bored, and unfulfilled at work [Blog post]. *Psychology Today.* Accessed at www.psychologytoday.com/ca/blog/career -transitions/201304/stuck-bored-and-unfulfilled-work on October 11, 2020.

Brown, B. (2007). *I thought it was just me (but it isn't): Making the journey from "What will people think?" to "I am enough."* New York: Gotham Books.

Brown, B. (2010). *The gifts of imperfection: Let go of who you think you're supposed to be and embrace who you are.* Center City, MN: Hazelden.

Brown, B. (2012). *Daring greatly: How the courage to be vulnerable transforms the way we live, love, parent, and lead.* New York: Gotham Books.

Brown, B. (2013, January 14). Shame v. guilt [Blog post]. *Brené Brown.* Accessed at https://brenebrown.com/blog/2013/01/14/shame-v-guilt on October 11, 2020.

Brown, B. (2015). *Rising strong: The reckoning, the rumble, the revolution.* New York: Penguin Random House.

Brown, B. (2017). *Braving the wilderness: The quest for true belonging and the courage to stand alone.* New York: Random House.

Brown, B. (2018). *Dare to lead: Brave work, tough conversations, whole hearts.* New York: Random House.

Brown, B. (2020). *List of values.* Accessed at https://daretolead.brenebrown.com /workbook-art-pics-glossary on November 15, 2020.

Brown, S. L., & Vaughan, C. (2009). *Play: How it shapes the brain, opens the imagination, and invigorates the soul.* New York: Avery.

Brunsting, N. C., Sreckovic, M. A., & Lane, K. L. (2014). Special education teacher burnout: A synthesis of research from 1979 to 2013. *Education and Treatment of Children, 37*(4), 681–711. Accessed at http://www.jstor.org/stable/44683943 on November 15, 2020.

Bubb, S., & Earley, P. (2004). *Managing teacher workload: Work-life balance and wellbeing.* Thousand Oaks, CA: SAGE.

Burgess, D. (2012). *Teach like a pirate: Increase student engagement, boost your creativity, and transform your life as an educator.* San Diego, CA: Dave Burgess Consulting.

Butler, R. (2012). Striving to connect: Extending an achievement goal approach to teacher motivation to include relational goals for teaching. *Journal of Educational Psychology, 104*(3), 726–742.

Butler, R., & Shibaz, L. (2014). Striving to connect and striving to learn: Influences of relational and mastery goals for teaching on teacher behaviors and student interest and help seeking. *International Journal of Educational Research, 65,* 41–53.

Camp, H. (2017). Goal setting as teacher development practice. *International Journal of Teaching and Learning in Higher Education, 29*(1), 61–72.

Canadian Improv Games. (2014). *Yes, and*. Accessed at https://improv.ca/yes-and on December 13, 2020.

Capaldi, C. A., Dopko, R. L., & Zelenski, J. M. (2014). The relationship between nature connectedness and happiness: A meta-analysis. *Frontiers in Psychology*, *5*(976).

Caputo, A. (2015). The relationship between gratitude and loneliness: The potential benefits of gratitude for promoting social bonds. *Europe's Journal of Psychology*, *11*(2), 323–334. Accessed at https://doi.org/10.5964/ejop.v11i2.826 on April 28, 2021.

Cardaciotto, L., Herbert, J. D., Forman, E. M., Moitra, E., & Farrow, V. (2008). The assessment of present-moment awareness and acceptance: The Philadelphia mindfulness scale. *Assessment*, *15*(2), 204–223.

Carrington, J. (2020). *Kids these days: A game plan for (re)connecting with those we teach, lead, and love*. San Diego, CA: IMPress.

Carrington, J. (2020, August 22). *Bring your brave* [Virtual conference presentation]. RELIT! 2020: Bring. Your. Brave.

Catmull, E., & Wallace, A. (2014). *Creativity, inc.: Overcoming the unseen forces that stand in the way of true inspiration*. New York: Random House.

Center on the Developing Child. (n.d.). *Topic: Toxic stress*. Accessed at https://developingchild.harvard.edu/resourcetag/toxic-stress on October 3, 2020.

Cheema, A., & Bagchi, R. (2011). The effect of goal visualization on goal pursuit: Implications for consumers and managers. *Journal of Marketing*, *75*(2), 109–123. Accessed at https://journals.sagepub.com/doi/10.1509/jm.75.2.109 on April 28, 2021.

Cherkowski, S., & Walker, K. (2013). Flourishing communities: Re-storying educational leadership using a positive research lens. *International Journal of Leadership in Education*, *17*(2), 200–216.

Cho, H., Pemberton, C. L., & Ray, B. (2017). An exploration of the existence, value and importance of creativity education. *Current Issues in Education*, *20*(1). Accessed at http://cie.asu.edu/ojs/index.php/cieatasu/article/view/1537 on April 28, 2021.

Chowdhury, M. R. (2020). *The science and psychology of goal-setting 101*. Accessed at https://positivepsychology.com/goal-setting-psychology on November 8, 2020.

Cigna. (2018). *Cigna's U.S. loneliness index: Survey of 20,000 Americans examining behaviors driving loneliness in the United States*. Accessed at www.multivu.com/players/English/8294451-cigna-us-loneliness-survey on June 5, 2020.

Cigna. (2020). *Cigna takes action to combat the rise of loneliness and improve mental wellness in America*. Accessed at www.cigna.com/newsroom/news-releases/2020/cigna-takes-action-to-combat-the-rise-of-loneliness-and-improve-mental-wellness-in-america on October 10, 2020.

Clear, J. (2020). *Core values list.* Accessed at https://jamesclear.com/core-values on November 15, 2020.

Cohen, S., Janicki-Deverts, D., & Miller, G. E. (2007). Psychological stress and disease. *Journal of the American Medical Association, 298*(14), 1685–1687.

Cohut, M. (2018). *What are the health benefits of being creative?* Accessed at www.medicalnewstoday.com/articles/320947 on November 29, 2020.

Coles, T. B. C. (2021). *Compassion fatigue and burnout: History, definitions, and assessment.* Accessed at www.dvm360.com/view/compassion-fatigue-and-burnout -history-definitions-and-assessment on July 20 , 2021.

Collaborative for Academic, Social, and Emotional Learning. (2012). *2013 CASEL guide: Effective social and emotional learning programs—Preschool and elementary school edition.* Chicago, IL: CASEL.

Collaborative for Academic, Social, and Emotional Learning. (2020). *SEL is . . . .* Accessed at https://casel.org/what-is-sel on April 28, 2021.

Columbia University, Teachers College. (2016). *Even Einstein struggled: Learning about scientists' failures can boost STEM grades.* Accessed at www.sciencedaily.com /releases/2016/05/160502084152.htm on October 1, 2020.

Covey, S. (1989). *The seven habits of highly effective people.* New York: Simon & Schuster.

Covey, S. R. (2004). *The seven habits of highly effective people: Restoring the character ethic* (Rev. ed.). New York: Free Press.

Cowley, G. (2003, February 23). Our bodies, our fears. *Newsweek.*

Cross, E. S., Kraemer, D. J. M., Hamilton, A. F. D. C., Kelley, W. M., & Grafton, S. T. (2009). Sensitivity of the action observation network to physical and observational learning. *Cerebral Cortex, 19*(2), 315–326. Accessed at doi: 10.1093 /cercor/bhn083 on April 28, 2021.

Csikszentmihalyi, M. (2004). *Flow, the secret to happiness* [Video file]. Accessed at www.ted.com/talks/mihaly_csikszentmihalyi_flow_the_secret_to_happiness? language=en on April 28, 2021.

Csikszentmihalyi, M. (2009). *Flow: The psychology of optimal experience.* New York: Harper & Row.

Csikszentmihalyi, M. (2013). *Creativity: The psychology of discovery and invention.* New York: HarperCollins. (Original work published 1996)

Darling-Hammond, L. (2001). The challenge of staffing our schools. *Educational Leadership, 58,* 12–17.

Darnon, C., Butera, F., & Harackiewicz, J. (2007). Achievement goals in social interactions: Learning with mastery vs. performance goals. *Motivation and Emotion, 31*(1), 61–70.

Day, C., & Gu, Q. (2014). *Resilient teachers, resilient schools: Building and sustaining quality in testing times.* New York: Routledge.

Delizonna, L. (2017). *High-performing teams need psychological safety: Here's how to create it*. Accessed at https://hbr.org/2017/08/high-performing-teams-need -psychological-safety-heres-how-to-create-it on December 12, 2020.

DiAngelo, R. J. (2018). *White fragility: Why it's so hard for white people to talk about racism*. Boston: Beacon Press.

Diaz-Varela, A., & Wright, L. H. V. (2019). Play for adults: Play-base approaches in teacher training. *Scottish Educational Review, 51*(2), 132–136.

Discovery Health Channel and American Psychological Association. (2020). *The road to resilience*. Accessed at https://www.uis.edu/counselingcenter/wp-content /uploads/sites/87/2013/04/the_road_to_resilience.pdf on July 25, 2021.

Doran, G. T. (1981). There's a S. M. A. R. T. way to write management's goals and objectives. *Management Review, 70*(11), 35–36.

Dowling, T. (2018). Compassion does not fatigue! *The Canadian Veterinary Journal (La Revue Veterinaire Canadienne), 59*(7), 749–750.

Duan, W., & Guo, P. (2015). Association between virtues and posttraumatic growth: Preliminary evidence from a Chinese community sample after earthquakes. *PeerJ, 3*, e883.

Dvir, Y., Ford, J., Hill, M., & Frazier, J. (2014). Childhood maltreatment, emotional dysregulation, and psychiatric comorbidities. *Harvard Review of Psychiatry, 22*(3), 149–161.

Dweck, C. S. (2006). *Mindset: The new psychology of success*. New York: Random House.

Dyson, B. G. (1991). *Secret formula for success: Vision, confidence and luck* [Commencement speech at Georgia Tech]. Atlanta, GA. Accessed https://www .markturner.net/wp-content/uploads/2015/05/Whistle-Brian_Dyson-Georgia _Tech_Commencement_Sept_1991-p3.pdf on November 4, 2020.

Eisenberger, N. I., & Cole, S. W. (2012). Social neuroscience and health: Neurophysiological mechanisms linking social ties with physical health. *Nature Neuroscience, 15*(5), 669–674. Accessed at PMID: 22504347 on April 28, 2021.

Eisenhower, D. D. (1954). *Address at the second assembly of the World Council of Churches* [Presidential address]. Evanston, IL. Accessed at www.presidency.ucsb .edu/node/232572 on April 28, 2021.

Emmons, R. A., Froh, J., & Rose, R. (2019). Gratitude. In M. W. Gallagher & S. J. Lopez (Eds.), *Positive psychological assessment: A handbook of models and measures* (pp. 317–332). Washington, DC: American Psychological Association.

Encyclopedia Britannica. (n.d.). *Alloying*. Accessed at www.britannica.com/science /metallurgy/Alloying on October 12, 2020.

Essa, H. (2018). *Your name is the key*! [Video file]. Accessed at www.ted.com/talks /huda_essa_your_name_is_the_key on April 28, 2021.

EssayHub. (n.d.). *Developing resilience: Overcoming and growing from setbacks.* Accessed at https://essayhub.net/essays/developing-resilienceovercoming-and -growing-from-setbacks on June 4, 2021.

Farber, N. (2012, April 19). The value of goals [Blog post]. *Psychology Today.* Accessed at www.psychologytoday.com/us/blog/the-blame-game/201204/the-value-goals on November 9, 2020.

Fattal, I. (2018). The value of failing. *The Atlantic.* Accessed at www.theatlantic.com /education/archive/2018/04/the-value-of-failing/558848 on October 1, 2020.

Fedewa, B. A., Burns, L. R., & Gomez, A. A (2005). Positive and negative perfectionism and the shame/guilt distinction: Adaptive and maladaptive characteristics. *Personality and Individual Differences, 38*(7), 1609–1619.

Ferris, T. (2014). *Ed Cooke, grandmaster of memory, on mental performance, imagination, and productive mischief* [Audio podcast]. Accessed at https:// tim.blog/2014/12/30/ed-cooke/ on June 11, 2021.

Fink, A. (2013). [Review of the book *The progress principle: Using small wins to ignite joy, engagement, and creativity at work* by T. Amabile & S. Kramer]. *Personnel Psychology, 66*(1), 292–294.

Fishman-Weaver, K. (2019). *How creating visual art contributes to SEL.* Accessed at www.edutopia.org/article/how-creating-visual-art-contributes-sel on November 28, 2020.

Flatow, I. (2013). *The myth of multitasking.* Accessed at www.npr.org/2013/05/10 /182861382/the-myth-of-multitasking on November 8, 2020.

Forgeard, M. J. C. (2015). *When, how, and for whom does creativity predict well-being?* Accessed at https://repository.upenn.edu/edissertations/1056 on April 28, 2021.

Frankl, V. E. (1984). *Man's search for meaning: An introduction to logotherapy.* New York: Simon & Schuster.

Fredrickson, B. L. (2013). Positive emotions broaden and build. *Advances in Experimental Social Psychology, 47,* 1–53.

Fredrickson, B. L., Tugade, M. M., Waugh, C. E., & Larkin, G. R. (2003). What good are positive emotions in crises? A prospective study of resilience and emotions following the terrorist attacks on the United State on September 11th, 2001. *Journal of Personality and Social Psychology, 84*(2), 365–376.

Frey, C. B., & Osborne, M. A. (2017). The future of employment: How susceptible are jobs to computerisation? *Technological Forecasting and Social Change, 114,* 254–280.

Fugate, J. M. B. (2013). Categorical perception for emotional faces. *Emotion Review, 5*(1), 84–89.

Galinsky, A. D., Magee, J. C., Inesi, M. E., & Gruenfeld, D. H. (2006). Power and perspectives not taken. *Psychological Science, 17*(12), 1068–1074.

Gan, Y. (2020). Happy people live longer and better: Advances in research on subjective well-being. *Applied Psychology: Health and Well-Being, 12*(1), 3–6.

Garcia, E., & Weiss, E. (2019). *U.S. schools struggle to hire and retain teachers.* Accessed at www.epi.org/publication/u-s-schools-struggle-to-hire-and-retain -teachers-the-second-report-in-the-perfect-storm-in-the-teacher-labor-market-series on April 29, 2021.

Garcia-Rill, E., Kezunovic, N., Hyde, J., Simon, C., Beck, P., & Urbano, F. J. (2013). Coherence and frequency in the reticular activating system (RAS). *Sleep medicine reviews, 17*(3), 227–238. Accessed at https://doi.org/10.1016/j.smrv.2012.06.002 on April 29, 2021.

Gardner, B., Lally, P., & Wardle, J. (2012). Making health habitual: The psychology of "habit-formation" and general practice. *British Journal of General Practice, 62*(605), 664–666.

Gazzara, K. (2010). *SMART goals history with Dr. George Doran* [Video file]. Accessed at www.youtube.com/watch?v=7LWbCqjLE-I on October 23, 2020.

Geher, G., Betancourt, K., & Jewell, O. (2017). The link between emotional intelligence and creativity. *Imagination, Cognition and Personality, 37*(1), 5–22.

Ghorpade, J., Lackritz, J., & Singh, G. (2007). Burnout and personality: Evidence from academia. *Journal of Career Assessment, 15*(2), 240–256.

Gibbs, S., & Miller, A. (2013). Teachers' resilience and well-being: A role for educational psychology. *Teachers and Teaching, 20*(5), 609–621.

Gilbert, E. (2015). *The flight of the hummingbird: The curiosity-driven life* [Video file]. Accessed at www.oprah.com/own-supersoulsessions/elizabeth-gilbert-the -curiosity-driven-life-video on December 12, 2020.

Gillespie, C. (2020). *What is toxic positivity—and why are experts saying it's dangerous right now?* Accessed at www.health.com/condition/infectious-diseases/coronavirus /what-is-toxic-positivity on April 29, 2021.

Gladwell, M. (2019). *Talking to strangers: What we should know about the people we don't know.* New York: Little, Brown, & Company.

Godin, S. (2007). *The dip: A little book that teaches you when to quit (and when to stick).* New York: Portfolio.

Godin, S. (2012). *Stop stealing dreams* [Video file]. Accessed at www.youtube.com /watch?v=sXpbONjV1Jc on April 29, 2021.

Godin, S. (2015). *Poke the box: When was the last time you did something for the first time?* New York: Penguin.

Gopnik, A., O'Grady, S., Lucas, C. G., Griffiths, T. L., Wente, A., Bridgers, S., et al. (2017). Changes in cognitive flexibility and hypothesis search across human life history from childhood to adolescence to adulthood. *Proceedings of the National Academy of Sciences of the United States of America, 114*(30), 7892–7899.

Gotlieb, R., Jahner, E., Immordino-Yang, M. H., & Kaufman, S. B. (2016). How social-emotional imagination facilitates deep learning and creativity in the classroom. In R. A. Beghetto & J. C. Kaufman (Eds.), *Nurturing creativity in the classroom* (2nd ed., pp. 308–336). Cambridge: Cambridge University Press.

Grant, A. (2013). *Give and take: A revolutionary approach to success.* New York: Viking.

Grant, A. (2016, January 16). Why I taught myself to procrastinate. *The New York Times.* Accessed at www.nytimes.com/2016/01/17/opinion/sunday/why-i-taught -myself-to-procrastinate.html on December 14, 2020.

Grant, A., & Sandberg, S. (2017). *Option b: Facing adversity, building resilience, and finding joy.* New York: Knopf.

Gross, J. J. (2015). Emotion regulation: Current status and future prospects. *Psychological Inquiry, 26*(1), 1–26.

Gross, J. J., & Levenson, R. W. (1997). Hiding feelings: The acute effects of inhibiting negative and positive emotion. *Journal of Abnormal Psychology, 106*(1), 95–103.

Groth, A. (2013). *SHERYL SANDBERG: Women need to get more comfortable with power.* Accessed at https://www.businessinsider.com.au/sheryl-sandberg-lean -in-2013-2 on December 14, 2020.

Gruener, B. (2019, March 12). Empathy to the rescue [Blog post]. *Character Strong.* Accessed at https://characterstrong.com/blog/121/empathy-to-the-rescue on November 22, 2020.

Grunschel, C., Patrzek, J., & Fries, S. (2012). Exploring reasons and consequences of academic procrastination: An interview study. *European Journal of Psychology of Education, 28*(3), 841–861.

Halifax, J. (2018). *Standing at the edge: Finding freedom where fear and courage meet.* New York: Flatiron Books.

Harmsen, R., Helms-Lorenz, M., Maulana, R., & van Veen, K. (2018). The relationship between beginning teachers' stress causes, stress responses, teaching behaviour and attrition. *Teachers and Teaching, 24*(6), 626–643.

Hartling, L. M., & Luchetta, T. (1999). Humiliation: Assessing the impact of derision, degradation, and debasement. *The Journal of Primary Prevention, 19*(4), 259–278.

Harvard Business Review. (2019). *To prevent burnout on your team, hold each other accountable.* Accessed at https://hbr.org/tip/2019/10/to-prevent-burnout-on-your -team-hold-each-other-accountable on November 9, 2020.

Haughey, D. (2014). *A brief history of SMART goals.* Accessed at www.projectsmart .co.uk/brief-history-of-smart-goals.php on October 27, 2020.

Heath, C., & Heath, D. (2017). *The power of moments: Why certain experiences have extraordinary impact.* New York: Simon & Schuster.

Herman, K. (2018). *More than 9 in 10 elementary school teachers feel highly stressed, MU study finds*. Accessed at https://munewsarchives.missouri.edu/news-releases /2018/0424-more-than-9-in-10 elementary-school-teachers-feel-highly-stressed -mu-study-finds/ on July 20, 2021.

Heyes, C. (2009). Where do mirror neurons come from? *Neuroscience & Biobehavioral Reviews, 34*(4), 575–583.

Hooker, T. (2020). *Stories of happiness, emotional goals and identity in 21st century teachers* [Thesis paper]. University of Waikato, Hamilton, New Zealand. Accessed at https://hdl.handle.net/10289/13765 on April 29, 2021.

Howells, K. (2014). An exploration of the role of gratitude in enhancing teacher– student relationships. *Teaching and Teacher Education, 42*, 58–67.

IBM. (n.d.). *IBM 2010 global CEO study: Creativity selected as most crucial factor for future success*. Accessed at https://www.ibm.com/news/ca/en/2010/05/20 /v384864m81427w34.html on November 29, 2020.

Iqbal, N., Anwar, S., & Haider, N. (2015). Effect of leadership style on employee performance. *Arabian Journal of Business and Management Review, 5*(5), 1–6.

Jackman, J. M., & Strober, M. H. (2003). Fear of feedback. *Harvard Business Review* Accessed at https://hbr.org/2003/04/fear-of-feedback on November 8, 2020.

Jaffe, E. (2011). *The psychological study of smiling*. Accessed at www .psychologicalscience.org/observer/the-psychological-study-of-smiling on November 22, 2020.

Jaffe, E. (2013). *Why wait? The science behind procrastination*. Accessed at www .psychologicalscience.org/observer/why-wait-the-science-behind-procrastination on April 29, 2021.

Janke, S., Nitsche, S., Praetorius, A., Benning, K., Fasching, M., Dresel, M., & Dickhauser, O. (2016). Deconstructing performance goal orientations: The merit of a dimensional approach. *Learning and Individual Differences, 50*, 133–146.

Jarvis, C. (2019). *Creative calling: Establish a daily practice, infuse your world with meaning, and find success in work, hobby, and life*. New York: HarperBusiness.

Jarvis, C. (2020). *Build a life you love w/ Chris Guillebeau*. Accessed at www .chasejarvis.com/blog/build-a-life-you-love-w-chris-guillebeau on November 8, 2020.

Jennings, P. A., & Greenberg, M. T. (2009). The prosocial classroom: Teacher social and emotional competence in relation to student and classroom outcomes. *Review of Educational Research, 79*(1), 491–525.

Juliani, A. (2013). *Why "20% time" is good for schools*. Accessed at www.edutopia.org /blog/20-percent-time-a-j-juliani on July 25, 2021.

Kabat-Zinn, J. (2018). *Falling awake: How to practice mindfulness in everyday life*. New York: Hachette Books.

Kaschka, W. P., Korczak, D., & Broich, K. (2011). Burnout: A fashionable diagnosis. *Deutsches Ärzteblatt Int, 108*(46), 781–787.

Kaufman, S. B., & Gregoire, C. (2015). *Wired to create: Unraveling the mysteries of the creative mind.* New York: Perigee Books.

Kelchtermans, G. (2017). "Should I stay or should I go?": Unpacking teacher attrition/retention as an educational issue. *Teachers and Teaching, 23*(8), 961–977.

Kelley, T., & Kelley, D. (2013). *Creative confidence.* New York: Crown Publishing Group.

Keltner, D. (2012). *The compassionate species.* Accessed at https://greatergood.berkeley .edu/article/item/the_compassionate_species on November 22, 2021.

Klauser, H. A. (2000). *Write it down, make it happen: Knowing what you want—and getting it!* New York: Scribner.

Kleingeld, A., van Mierlo, H., & Arends, L. (2011). The effect of goal setting on group performance: A meta-analysis. *Journal of Applied Psychology, 96*(6), 1289–1304.

Klingsieck, K. B. (2013). Procrastination: When good things don't come to those who wait. *European Psychologist, 18*(1), 24–34.

Kobasa, S. C. (1979). Stressful life events, personality, and health: An inquiry into hardiness. *Journal of Personality and Social Psychology, 37*(1), 1.

Koller, J. R., & Bertel, J. M. (2006). Responding to today's mental health needs of children, families and schools: Revisiting the preservice training and preparation of school-based personnel. *Education & Treatment of Children, 29,* 197–217.

Konnikova, M. (2016). How people learn to become resilient. *New Yorker.* Accessed at www.newyorker.com/science/maria-konnikova/the-secret-formula-for-resilience on October 12, 2020.

Kraft, H. (2020). *Deep kindness: Practicing kindness in a world that oversimplifies it.* New York: Tiller Press.

Kresser, C. (2017). *Batching: A simple strategy for boosting brainpower and increasing productivity.* Accessed at https://kresserinstitute.com/batching-simple-strategy -boosting-brainpower-increasing-productivity on November 8, 2020.

Krockow, E. (2018). How many decisions do we make each day? [Blog post]. *Psychology Today.* Accessed at www.psychologytoday.com/us/blog/stretching-theory/201809 /how-many-decisions-do-we-make-each-day on November 16, 2020.

Kross, E., Berman, M. G., Mischel, W., Smith, E. E., & Wager, T. D. (2011). Social rejection shares somatosensory representations with physical pain. *Proceedings of the National Academy of Sciences of the United States of America, 108*(15), 6270–6275.

Kuehn, P. D. (2013). *Cultural coping strategies and their connection to grief therapy modalities for children: An investigation into current knowledge and practice.* Accessed at https://sophia.stkate.edu/msw_papers/215 on April 29, 2021.

Kunter, M., & Holzberger, D. (2014). Loving teaching: Research on teachers' intrinsic orientations. In P. W. Anderson, S. A. Karabenick, & H. M. G. Watt (Eds.), *Teacher motivation: Theory and practice* (pp. 83–99). New York: Routledge.

Lambert, N. M., Clark, M. S., Durtschi, J., Fincham, F. D., & Graham, S. M. (2010). Benefits of expressing gratitude: Expressing gratitude to a partner changes one's view of the relationship. *Psychological Science, 21*(4), 574–580.

Lamott, A. (1995). *Bird by bird: Some instructions on writing and life.* New York: Anchor Books.

Lavy, S., & Bocker, S. (2017). A path to teacher happiness? A sense of meaning affects teacher-student relationships, which affect job satisfaction. *Journal of Happiness Studies, 19*, 1485–1503.

Levitin, D. (2014, August 9). Hit the reset button in your brain. *The New York Times.* Accessed at https://www.nytimes.com/2014/08/10/opinion/sunday/hit-the-reset -button-in-your-brain.html on June 3, 2021.

Li, Y., Hassett, A. L., & Seng, J. S. (2018). Exploring the mutual regulation between oxytocin and cortisol as a marker of resilience. *Archives of Psychiatric Nursing, 33*(2), 164–173.

Lieberman, M. D. (2015). *Social: Why our brains are wired to connect.* Oxford: Oxford University Press.

Locke, E. A., & Latham, G. P. (2002). Building a practically useful theory of goal setting and task motivation: A 35-year odyssey. *American Psychologist, 57*(9), 705–717.

Locke, E. A., & Latham, G. P. (2019). The development of goal setting theory: A half century retrospective. *Motivation Science, 5*(2), 93–105.

Loh, K. K., & Kanai, R. (2016). How has the internet reshaped human cognition? *Neuroscientist, 22*(5), 506–520.

Lynch, J., Prihodova, L., Dunne, P. J., Carroll, A., Walsh, C., McMahon, G., et al. (2018). Mantra meditation for mental health in the general population: A systematic review. *European Journal of Integrative Medicine, 23*, 101–108.

MacKay, J. (2019, March 20). Screen time stats 2019: Here's how much you use your phone during the workday [Blog post]. *RescueTime.* Accessed at https://blog.rescuetime.com/screen-time-stats-2018 on December 13, 2020.

MacKenzie, T., & Bathurst-Hunt, R. (2019). *Inquiry mindset.* La Vergne: Elevate Books Edu.

Madanes, C. (2016). *The 6 human needs for fulfillment.* Accessed at https://cloemadanes.com/2016/10/12/the-6-human-needs-for-fulfillment on April 29, 2021.

Mahmoodi-Shahrebabaki, M. (2016). The effect of perfectionism on burnout among English language teachers: The mediating role of anxiety. *Teachers and Teaching, 23*(1), 91–105.

Malin, H. (2018). *Teaching for purpose: Preparing students for lives of meaning.* Cambridge, MA: Harvard Education Press.

Mansfield, C. F., & Beltman, S. (2014). Teacher motivation from a goal content perspective: Beginning teachers' goals for teaching. *International Journal of Educational Research, 65,* 54–64.

Mansfield, C., & Beltman, S. (2019). Promoting resilience for teachers: Pre-service and in-service professional learning. *The Australian Educational Researcher, 46,* 583–588.

Mansfield, C. F., Beltman, S., Broadley, T., & Weatherby-Fell, N. (2016). Building resilience in teacher education: An evidenced informed framework. *Teaching and Teacher Education, 54,* 77–87.

Mansfield, C., Beltman, S., Weatherby-Fell, N., & Broadley, T. (2016). *Classroom ready? Buildling resilience in teacher education.* In R. Brandenburg, S. McDonough, J. Burke, & S. White (Eds.), *Teacher education: Innovation, intervention and impact* (pp. 211–229). Singapore: Springer.

Mart, C. T. (2018). A passionate teacher: Teacher commitment and dedication to student learning. *International Journal of Academic Research in Progressive Education and Development, 2*(1), 437–442.

Maslach, C., & Florian, V. (1988). Burnout, job setting, and self-evaluation among rehabilitation counselors. *Rehabilitation Psychology, 33*(2), 85–93.

Maslach, C., & Leiter, M. P. (2016). Understanding the burnout experience: Recent research and its implications for psychiatry. *World Psychiatry, 15*(2), 103–111.

Maslow, A. H. (1943). A theory of human motivation. *Psychological Review, 50*(4), 370–396.

Massimiliano, P. (2015). The effects of age on divergent thinking and creative objects production: A cross-sectional study. *High Ability Studies, 26*(1), 93–104.

Matei, A. (2019). *Shock! Horror! Do you know how much time you spend on your phone?* Accessed at www.theguardian.com/lifeandstyle/2019/aug/21/cellphone-screen -time-average-habits on December 13, 2020.

Matthews, D. (2019). Empathy: Where kindness, compassion, and happiness begin. [Blog post]. *Psychology Today.* Accessed at www.psychologytoday.com/ca/blog/ going-beyond-intelligence/201910/empathy-where-kindness-compassion-and- happiness-begin on November 22, 2020.

Matthews, G. (2015). *Goal research summary.* Paper presented at the 9th Annual International Conference of the Psychology Research Unit of Athens Institute for Education and Research (ATINER), Athens, Greece.

McDaniel, R. (2016, June 30). Goal-setter or problem solver? *HuffPost*. Accessed at www.huffpost.com/entry/goal-setter-or-problem-so_b_7543084 on November 8, 2020.

McKeown, G. (2014). *Essentialism: The disciplined pursuit of less*. New York: Crown Business.

McKibben, S. (2014). The two-minute relationship builder. *Education Update, 56*(7). Accessed at www.ascd.org/publications/newsletters/education_update/jul14/vol56 /num07/The_Two-Minute_Relationship_Builder.aspx#:~:text= on April 29, 2021.

McLeod, S. A. (2020). *Maslow's hierarchy of needs*. Accessed at www .simplypsychology.org/maslow.html on April 29, 2021.

McQuaid, M. (2018, April 19). Could compassion fuel your success? [Blog post]. *Psychology Today*. Accessed at www.psychologytoday.com/intl/blog/functioning -flourishing/201804/could-compassion-fuel-your-success on November 22, 2021.

Meichenbaum, D. (2006). Resilience and posttraumatic growth: A constructive narrative perspective. In L. G. Calhoun & R. G. Tedeschi (Eds.), *Handbook of posttraumatic growth: Research and practice* (pp. 355–368). Mahwah, NJ: Lawrence Erlbaum Associates.

Mehta, M. (2013). *Why our brains like short-term goals*. Accessed at www .entrepreneur.com/article/225356 on April 29, 2021.

MentalHelp. (n.d.). *The maintenance of anxiety disorders: Maladaptive coping strategies*. Accessed at www.mentalhelp.net/anxiety/maladaptive-coping-strategies on October 11, 2020.

Michael, M. (2018a). *Can you teach kindness and empathy? Actionable proven tips you can implement in your class starting today (with Barbara Gruener)* [Audio podcast]. KindSight101.

Michael, M. (2018b). *How to avoid educator burnout: Nourishing teacher well-being through mindful practice (with Lisa Baylis)* [Audio podcast]. KindSight101.

Michael, M. (2018c). *The five steps for teaching self-regulation and reducing flight, fight, freeze responses in the classroom (with Dr. Stuart Shanker)* [Audio podcast]. KindSight101.

Michael, M. (2018d). *How to overcome empathic burnout (with Dr. Rebecca Alber)* [Audio podcast]. KindSight 101.

Michael, M. (2018e). *The dark side of growth mindset (with Stefanie Faye Frank)* [Audio podcast]. KindSight 101.

Michael, M. (2018f). *What is school for (with Seth Godin)* [Audio podcast]. KindSight 101.

Michael, M. (2019a). *Five reasons kindness is hard and how to make it easy (with Houston Kraft)* [Audio podcast]. KindSight101.

Michael, M. (2019b). *How to be a connection ninja (with David Knapp-Fisher)* [Audio podcast]. KindSight101.

Michael, M. (2019c). *How to build trust in hostile environments (with Dr. Darryl Stickel)* [Audio podcast]. KindSight101.

Michael, M. (2019d). *How to magically connect with anyone (with Brian Miller)* [Audio podcast]. KindSight101.

Michael, M. (2019e). *Kindness, superheroes, and DNA (with Laurie McIntosh)* [Audio podcast]. KindSight101.

Michael, M. (2019f). *The Dope Educator (with David Jay)* [Audio podcast]. KindSight101.

Michael, M. (2019g). *The Kindness Ninjas (with Allie Apels)* [Audio podcast]. KindSight101.

Michael, M (2019h). *Choose to rise (with Janelle Morrison)* [Audio podcast]. KindSight 101.

Miller, B. (2018). *Three new people: Make the most of your daily interactions and stop missing amazing opportunities.* All Things Publishing.

Miller, K., & McGowan, A. (2014). *The new science behind early education* [Blog post]. Accessed at http://blogs.wgbh.org/innovation-hub/2014/1/31/new-science-behind -early-education on September 19, 2020.

MindTools. (n.d.a.). *Developing resilience: Overcoming and growing from setbacks.* Accessed at www.mindtools.com/pages/article/resilience.htm on October 13, 2020.

MindTools. (n.d.b.). *Personal goal setting: Planning to live your life your way.* Accessed at www.mindtools.com/page6.html on November 8, 2020.

MindTools. (n.d.c.). *SMART goals: How to make your goals achievable.* Accessed at www.mindtools.com/pages/article/smart-goals.htm on November 8, 2020.

Mineo, D. L. (2014). The importance of trust in leadership. *Research Management Review, 20*(1), 1–6.

Moeller, A. J., Theiler, J. M., & Wu, C. (2011). Goal setting and student achievement: A longitudinal study. *The Modern Language Journal, 96*(2), 153–169.

Molnar-Szakacs, I., Wu, A. D., Robles, F. J., & Iacoboni, M. (2007). Do you see what I mean? Corticospinal excitability during observation of culture-specific gestures. *PLoS One, 2*(7), 626.

Moran, S. (2018). Purpose-in-action education: Introduction and implications. *Journal of Moral Education, 47*(2), 145–158.

Morisano, D., Hirsh, J. B., Peterson, J. B., Pihl, R. O., & Shore, B. M. (2010). Setting, elaborating, and reflecting on personal goals improves academic performance. *Journal of Applied Psychology, 95*(2), 255–264.

Moser, J. S., Schroder, H. S., Heeter, C., Moran, T. P., & Lee, Y. H. (2011). Mind your errors: Evidence for a neural mechanism linking growth mind-set to adaptive posterror adjustments. *Psychological Science, 22*(12), 1484–1489.

Nagoski, E., & Nagoski, A. (2019). *Burnout: The secret to unlocking the stress cycle.* New York: Ballantine Books.

Najavits, L. M. (2002). *Seeking safety: A treatment manual for PTSD and substance abuse.* New York: Guilford Press.

National Institute of Mental Health (2021). *Mental illness.* Accessed at www.nimh .nih.gov/health/statistics/mental-illness.shtml on October 3, 2020.

Neff, K. (2011). *Self-compassion: Stop beating yourself up and leave insecurity behind.* New York: William Morrow.

Neff, K. (2021). *The compassionate instinct.* Accessed at https://greatergood.berkeley .edu/article/item/the_compassionate_instinct on July 20, 2021.

Nesse, R. M., Bhatnagar, S., & Ellis, B. (2016). Evolutionary origins and functions of the stress response system. In G. Fink (Ed.), *Stress: Concepts, cognition, emotion, and behavior* (pp. 95–101). London: Elsevier Inc.

Nin, A. (1961). *Seduction of the minotaur.* Denver, CO: A. Swallow.

Noyes, C. E. (1907). *The gate of appreciation: Studies in the relation of art to life.* Boston: Houghton, Mifflin and Company.

Oberle, E., & Schonert-Reichl, K. A. (2016). Stress contagion in the classroom? The link between classroom teacher burnout and morning cortisol in elementary school students. *Social Science & Medicine, 159,* 30–37.

O'Brien, J., Pearpoint, J., & Kahn, L. (2015). *The path and maps handbook: Person-centered ways to build community.* Toronto, ON: Inclusion Press.

Online Etymology Dictionary. (n.d.). *Compassion.* Accessed at www.etymonline.com /word/compassion on November 22, 2020.

Paulick, I., Retelsdorf, J., & Möller, J. (2013). Motivation for choosing teacher education: Associations with teachers' achievement goals and instructional practices. *International Journal of Educational Research, 61,* 60–70.

Paz, Z. (n.d.). *Famous people with dyslexia: Sir Richard Branson dyslexia coping tips.* Accessed at www.ldrfa.org/famous-people-with-dyslexia-sir-richard-branson -dyslexia-coping-tips on October 12, 2020.

Petriglieri, G. (2018). *To take charge of your career, start by building your tribe.* Accessed at https://hbr.org/2018/04/to-take-charge-of-your-career-start-by -building-your-tribe on December 15, 2020.

Pfeffer, J., & Sutton, R. I. (2000). *The knowing-doing gap: How smart companies turn knowledge into action.* Boston: Harvard Business School Press.

Pink, D. H. (2009). *Drive: The surprising truth about what motivates us.* New York: Riverhead Books.

Pink, D. H. (2016). *2016 Georgetown commencement speech* [Video file]. Accessed at www.danpink.com/resource/2016-georgetown-commencement-speech on November 22, 2020.

Pink, D. H. (2018). *When: The scientific secrets of perfect timing.* New York: Riverhead Books.

Piper, W. T., Saslow, L. R., & Saturn, S. R. (2015). Autonomic and prefrontal events during moral elevation. *Biological Psychology, 108,* 51–55.

Platek, B. (2008). *Through a glass darkly: Miriam Greenspan on moving from grief to gratitude.* Accessed at https://www.thesunmagazine.org/issues/385/through-a -glass-darkly on April 30, 2021.

Poortvliet, P., & Darnon, C. (2013). Understanding positive attitudes toward helping peers: The role of mastery goals and academic self-efficacy. *Self and Identity, 13*(3), 345–363.

Porath, C. (2016). *Mastering civility: A manifesto for the workplace.* New York: Grand Central Publishing.

Porath, C. (2018). *Why being respectful to your coworkers is good for business* [Video file]. Accessed at www.ted.com/talks/christine_porath_why_being_respectful_to_your _coworkers_is_good_for_business/footnotes?language=en on April 29, 2021.

Quintero, S. (n.d.). *Toxic positivity: The dark side of positive vibes.* Accessed at https:// thepsychologygroup.com/toxic-positivity on October 11, 2020.

Robbins, M. (2017). *The 5 second rule: Transform your life, work, and confidence with everyday courage.* Boston: Mel Robbins Productions.

Robbins, T. (n.d.). *What is priming? How can I use priming psychology?* Accessed at www.tonyrobbins.com/ask-tony/priming on January 18, 2021.

Robinson, K. (2006). *Do schools kill creativity?* [Video file]. Accessed at www.ted.com /talks/sir_ken_robinson_do_schools_kill_creativity on December 12, 2020.

Rodriguez, T. (2013). *Negative emotions are key to well-being.* Accessed at www .scientificamerican.com/article/negative-emotions-key-well-being on October 11, 2020.

Rosen, J. B., & Donley, M. P. (2006). Animal studies of amygdala function in fear and uncertainty: Relevance to human research. *Biological Psychology, 73*(1), 49–60.

Roth, S., Newman, E., Pelcovitz, D., van der Kolk, B., & Mandel, F. S. (1997). Complex PTSD in victims exposed to sexual and physical abuse: Results from the DSM-IV field trial for posttraumatic stress disorder. *Journal Traumatic Stress, 10*(4), 539–555.

Rowland, L. (2018). Kindness: Society's golden chain. *The Psychologist, 31,* 30–35.

Rubin, G. (2017). *The Four Tendencies: The indispensable personality profiles that reveal how to make your life better (and other people's lives better, too).* New York: Harmony.

Rubin, G. (2019). *Outer order inner calm: Declutter and organize to make more room for happiness.* New York: Harmony.

Rubin, R. S. (2002). Will the real SMART goals please stand up? *The Industrial-Organizational Psychologist, 39*(4), 26–27.

Ryback, R. The science of accomplishing your goals [Blog post]. *Psychology Today*. Accessed at www.psychologytoday.com/ca/blog/the-truisms-wellness/201610 /the-science-accomplishing-your-goals on April 30, 2021.

Salzberg, S. (1995). *Lovingkindness: The revolutionary art of happiness*. Boston: Shambhala.

Salzberg, S. (2014). *Real happiness at work: Meditations for accomplishment, achievement, and peace*. New York: Workman Publishing Company, Inc.

Sansone, R. A., & Sansone, L. A. (2010). Gratitude and well-being: The benefits of appreciation. *Psychiatry*, *7*(11), 18–22.

Santoro, D. A. (2018). *Demoralized: Why teachers leave the profession they love and how they can stay*. Cambridge, MA: Harvard Education Press.

Saraiya, T., & Lopez-Castro, T. (2016). Ashamed and afraid: A scoping review of the role of shame in post-traumatic stress disorder (PTSD). *Journal of Clinical Medicine*, *5*(11), 94.

Schiefele, U., & Schaffner, E. (2015). Teacher interests, mastery goals, and self-efficacy as predictors of instructional practices and student motivation. *Contemporary Educational Psychology*, *42*, 159–171.

Schwingshackl, A. (2014). The fallacy of chasing after work-life balance. *Frontiers in Pediatrics*, *2*(26).

Schonert-Reichl, K. A. (2017). Social and emotional learning and teachers. *JSTOR*, *27*(1), 137–155.

Schulte, B. (2014). *Overwhelmed: Work, love, and play when no one has the time*. New York: Sarah Crichton Books.

Schultz, W. (2002). Getting formal with dopamine and reward. *Neuron*, *36*(2), 241–263.

Seelig, T. (2013). *5 ways to innovate by cross-pollinating ideas*. Accessed at www .fastcompany.com/1672519/5-ways-to-innovate-by-cross-pollinating-ideas on December 15, 2020.

Seifert, K., & Sutton, R (2009). *Educational psychology* (2nd ed.). The Saylor Foundation. Accessed at www.saylor.org/site/wp-content/uploads/2012/06 /Educational-Psychology.pdf on April 30, 2021.

Seligman, M. E. (2006). *Learned optimism: How to change your mind and your life*. New York: Vintage Books.

Seligman, M. E. (2011). *Flourish: A visionary new understanding of happiness and well-being*. New York: Free Press.

Seppälä, E. (2017). *The happiness track*. New York: HarperCollins.

Seppälä, E., Bradley, C., & Goldstein, M. R. (2020). *Research: Why breathing is so effective at reducing stress*. Accessed at https://hbr.org/2020/09/research-why -breathing-is-so-effective-at-reducing-stress on October 11, 2020.

Seppälä, E., & Cameron, K. (2015). *Proof that positive work cultures are more productive.* Accessed at https://hbr.org/2015/12/proof-that-positive-work-cultures-are-more-productive on April 30, 2021.

Seppälä, E., & Moeller, E. (2018). *1 in 5 employees is highly engaged and at the risk of burnout.* Accessed at https://hbr.org/2018/02/1-in-5-highly-engaged-employees-is-at-risk-of-burnout on September 20, 2020.

Shamay-Tsoory, S. G., Saporta, N., Marton-Alper, I. Z., & Gvirts, H. Z. (2019). Herding brains: A core neural mechanism for social alignment. *Trends in Cognitive Sciences, 23*(3), 174–186.

Shanker, S. (2017). *Self-reg: How to help your child (and you) break the stress cycle and successfully engage with life.* Penguin Canada.

Shatté, A. (2015). *5 ways to cure chronic procrastination.* Accessed at www.inc.com/andrew-shatte/5-ways-to-cure-chronic-procrastination.html on November 9, 2020.

Shen, L. (2018). The evolution of shame and guilt. *PLOS One, 13*(7).

Shonkoff, J. P., & Garner, A. S. (2012). The lifelong effects of early childhood adversity and toxic stress. *Pediatrics, 129*(1), 232–246.

Shorosh, S., & Berkovich, I. (2020). The relationships between workgroup emotional climate and teachers' burnout and coping style. *Research Papers in Education.*

Siegel, D. (2014). *Daniel Siegel: Name it to tame it* [Video file]. Accessed at www.youtube.com/watch?v=ZcDLzppD4Jc on July 20, 2021.

Simons, D. J., & Chabris, C. F. (2010). *The invisible gorilla: And other ways our intuitions deceive us.* New York: Crown.

Simpson, W. K., & Pychyl, T. A. (2009). In search of the arousal procrastinator: Investigating the relation between procrastination, arousal-based personality traits and beliefs about motivations. *Personality and Individual Differences, 47*(8), 906–911.

Sinek, S. (2009). *Start with why: How great leaders inspire everyone to take action.* New York: Portfolio.

Sinek, S. (2014). *Leaders eat last: Why some teams pull together and others don't.* New York: Penguin Group.

Sisgold, S. (2013, June 4). Limited beliefs: The buzz killer [Blog post]. *Psychology Today.* Accessed at www.psychologytoday.com/blog/life-in-body/201306 on April 30, 2021.

Skinner, E., & Beers, J. (2016) Mindfulness and teachers' coping in the classroom: A developmental model of teacher stress, coping, and everyday resilience. In K. A. Schonert-Reichl & R. W. Roeser (Eds.), *Mindfulness in behavioral health. Handbook of mindfulness in education: Integrating theory and research into practice* (pp. 99–118). Berlin: Springer-Verlag.

Slavich, G. M., & Irwin, M. R. (2014). From stress to inflammation and major depressive disorder: A social signal transduction theory of depression. *Psychological Bulletin, 140*(3),774–815.

Slavich, G. M., O'Donovan, A., Epel, E. S., & Kemeny, M. E. (2010). Black sheep get the blues: A psychobiological model of social rejection and depression. *Neuroscience and Biobehavioral Reviews, 35*(1), 39–45.

Smith, N. (2018). *Zero-sum thinking makes our fights much nastier.* Accessed at www.bloomberg.com/opinion/articles/2018–02–12/zero-sum-thinking-makes-our-fights-much-nastier on November 22, 2020.

Soon, C. S., Brass, M., Heinze, H., & Haynes, J. (2008). Unconscious determinants of free decisions in the human brain. *Nature Neuroscience, 11*(5), 543–545.

Stahl, A. (2018). *Here's how creativity actually improves your health.* Accessed at www.forbes.com/sites/ashleystahl/2018/07/25/heres-how-creativity-actually-improves-your-health/?sh=48b24bdb13a6 on November 29, 2020.

Steel, P. (2007). The nature of procrastination: A meta-analytic and theoretical review of quintessential self-regulatory failure. *Psychological Bulletin, 133*(1), 65–94.

Steel, P. (2011). *The procrastination equation: How to stop putting stuff off and start getting things done.* New York: Harper.

Steers, M. N., Quist, M. C., Bryan, J. L., Foster, D. W., Young, C. M., & Neighbors, C. (2016). I want you to like me: Extraversion, need for approval, and time on Facebook as predictors of anxiety. *Translational Issues in Psychological Science, 2*(3), 283–293.

Suárez-Orozco, C., Casanova, S., Martin, M., Katsiaficas, D., Vuellar, V., Smith, N. A., et al. (2015). Toxic rain in class: Classroom interpersonal microaggressions. *Educational Researcher, 44*(3), 151–160.

Summerville, A. (2019, March 21). Is comparison really the thief of joy? [Blog post]. *Psychology Today.* Accessed at www.psychologytoday.com/ca/blog/multiple-choice/201903/is-comparison-really-the-thief-joy on December 12, 2020.

Suttie, J. (2016). *How to listen to pain: A Q&A with Brené Brown about her new book, Rising Strong.* Accessed at https://greatergood.berkeley.edu/article/item/how_to_listen_to_pain#:~:text=According%20to%20Bren%C3%A9%20Brown%2C%20a,we%20interact%20in%20the%20world On October 11, 2020.

Tay, L., & Diener, E. (2011). Needs and subjective well-being around the world. *Journal of Personality and Social Psychology, 101*(2), 354–356.

Tedeschi, R. G., & Calhoun, L. G. (1996). The posttraumatic growth inventory: Measuring the positive legacy of trauma. *Journal of Traumatic Stress, 9*(3), 455–471.

Thayer, R. E. (1996). *The origin of everyday moods: Managing energy, tension, and stress.* Oxford University Press.

Thayer, R. E., Peters, D. P. III, Takahashi, P. J., & Birkhead-Flight, A. M. (1993). Mood and behavior (smoking and sugar snacking) following moderate exercise: A partial test of self-regulation theory. *Personality and Individual Differences, 14*(1), 97–104.

The Script. (2012). *Hall of fame* [Song lyrics]. Danny O'Donoghue.

The Zones of Regulation. (n.d.). *Free downloadable handouts.* Accessed at www
.zonesofregulation.com/free-downloadable-handouts.html on October 12, 2020.

Thompson, J. (2012, September 9). Mimicry and mirroring can be good or bad
[Blog post]. *Psychology Today.* Accessed at www.psychologytoday.com/ca/blog
/beyond-words/201209/mimicry-and-mirroring-can-be-good-or-bad on
November 22, 2021.

Thomsen, B. (Ed.). (2003). *The man in the arena: The selected writings of Theodore
Roosevelt; a reader.* New York: Forge.

Tough, P. (2011, September 14). What if the secret to success is failure? *The New York
Times.* Accessed at www.nytimes.com/2011/09/18/magazine/what-if-the-secret-to
-success-is-failure.html on August 13, 2021.

Travis, J. (2004). *Fear not: Scientists are learning how people can unlearn fear.* Accessed
at www.sciencenews.org/article/fear-not on April 30, 2021.

Umphrey, L. R., & Sherblom, J. C. (2018). The constitutive relationship of listening
to hope, emotional intelligence, stress, and life satisfaction. *International Journal
of Listening, 32*(1), 24–48.

University of California. (2016–2017). *SMART goals: A how to guide.* Accessed at
www.ucop.edu/local-human-resources/_files/performance-appraisal/How%20
to%20write%20SMART%20Goals%20v2.pdf on April 30, 2021.

University of the Sunshine Coast. (n.d.). *Reframing your thinking.* Accessed at www
.usc.edu.au/media/3850/Reframingyourthinking.pdf on October 12, 2020.

Vandraiss, K. (2017, February 27). How perfectionism hurts you. *SUCCESS.*
Accessed at www.success.com/how-perfectionism-hurts-you on October 11, 2020.

Vengapally, M. (2019). *Work-life balance is impossible: Here's what to strive for instead.*
Accessed at www.forbes.com/sites/allbusiness/2019/02/06/work-life-balance-is
-impossible on November 16, 2020.

Vesely, A. K., Saklofske, D. H., & Leschied, A. D. W. (2013). Teachers—the vital
resource: The contribution of emotional intelligence to teacher efficacy and well-
being. *Canadian Journal of School Psychology, 28*(1), 71–89.

Vitale, J. L. (2011). Formal and informal music learning: Attitudes and perspectives
of secondary school non-music teachers. *International Journal of Humanities and
Social Science, 1*(5), 1–14.

Wadsworth, M. E. (2015). Development of maladaptive coping: A functional
adaptation to chronic, uncontrollable stress. *Child Development Perspectives, 9*(2),
96–100.

Wahba, M. A., & Bridwell, L. G. (1976). Maslow reconsidered: A review of research
on the need hierarchy theory. *Organizational Behavior and Human Performance,
15*(2), 212–240.

Weingarden, H., Renshaw, K. D., Wilhelm, S., Tangney, J. P., & DiMauro, J. (2016). Anxiety and shame as risk factors for depression, suicidality, and functional impairment in body dysmorphic disorder and obsessive compulsive disorder. *The Journal of Nervous and Mental Disease, 204*(11), 832–839.

Weze, C., Leathard, H. L., Grange, J., Tiplady, P., & Stevens, G. (2007). Healing by gentle touch ameliorates stress and other symptoms in people suffering with mental health disorders or psychological stress. *Evidence-Based Complementary and Alternative Medicine, 4*(1), 115–123.

Wharton. (2014). *Can creativity be taught?* Accessed at https://knowledge.wharton.upenn.edu/article/can-creativity-be-taught on October 11, 2020.

Whillans, A. (2020). *Time smart: How to reclaim your time and live a happier life.* Boston: Harvard Business Review Press.

Whitbourne, S. K. (2018, January 9). A new way to understand procrastination [Blog post]. *Psychology Today.* Accessed at www.psychologytoday.com/ca/blog/fulfillment-any-age/201801/new-way-understand-procrastination on November 9, 2020.

Wieth, M. B., & Zacks, R. T. (2011). Time of day effects on problem solving: When the non-optimal is optimal. *Thinking & Reasoning, 17*(4), 387–401.

Wiktionary. (n.d.). *Sonder.* Accessed at en.wiktionary.org/wiki/sonder on April 30, 2021.

World Health Organization. (2017). *Depression and other common mental disorders.* Accessed at www.who.int/publications/i/item/depression-global-health-estimates on November 22, 2020.

Wróbel, M. (2013). Can empathy lead to emotional exhaustion in teachers? The mediating role of emotional labor. *International Journal of Occupational Medicine and Environmental Health, 26*(4), 581–592.

Yenigun, S. (2014). *Play doesn't end with childhood: Why adults need recess too.* Accessed at www.npr.org/sections/ed/2014/08/06/336360521/play-doesnt-end-with-childhood-why-adults-need-recess-too on December 15, 2020.

Yin, H.-B., Chi-Kin Lee, J.-L., Jin, Y.-H., & Zhang, Z. (2012). The effect of trust on teacher empowerment: The mediation of teacher efficacy. *Educational Studies, 39*(1), 13–28.

Younger, R. (2019). *Be, awake, create: Mindful practices to spark creativity.* Oakland, CA: New Harbinger.

Zaki, J. (2016). *Kindness contagion.* Accessed at www.scientificamerican.com/article/kindness-contagion on November 22, 2020.

Index

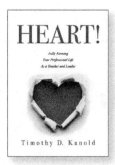

HEART!
Timothy D. Kanold

Explore the concept of a heartprint—the distinctive impression an educator's heart leaves on students and colleagues during his or her professional career. Use this resource to reflect on your professional journey and discover how to increase efficacy, and foster productive, heart-centered classrooms and schools.
BKF749

SOUL!
Timothy D. Kanold

Chart a deeply rewarding journey toward discovering your soul story—the pursuit of your moral good, to create good in others. Refreshing and uplifting, this resource includes dozens of real stories from educators, as well as ample space for journaling and self-reflection.
BKF982

180 Days of Self-Care for Busy Educators
Tina H. Boogren

Rely on *180 Days of Self-Care for Busy Educators* to help you lead a happier, healthier more fulfilled life inside and outside of the classroom. With Tina H. Boogren's guidance, you will work through 36 weeks of self-care strategies during the school year.
BKF920

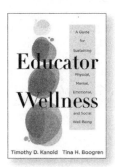

Educator Wellness
Timothy D. Kanold & Tina H. Boogren

Educator and teacher self-care can be challenging, but embracing a holistic health and wellness plan can improve your physical, mental, emotional, and social well-being both inside and outside of school. This reflective journal provides the ideas and guidance you need to support you on your wellness journey.
BKG053

"Tremendous, tremendous, tremendous!

The speaker made me do some very deep internal reflection about the **PLC process** and the personal responsibility I have in making the school improvement process work **for ALL kids**."

—Marc Rodriguez, teacher effectiveness coach,
Denver Public Schools, Colorado

PD Services

Our experts draw from decades of research and their own experiences to bring you practical strategies for building and sustaining a high-performing PLC. You can choose from a range of customizable services, from a one-day overview to a multiyear process.

Book your PLC PD today!
888.763.9045

Solution Tree